steam cooking

steam cooking

Jenny Stacey

A QUINTET BOOK

Published by the Apple Press
Sheridan House
112-116A Western Road
Hove
East Sussex BN3 1DU

ISBN 1 840923 27 X

Reprinted 2000, 2001, 2002

This book was designed and produced by
Quintet Publishing Limited
6 Blundell Street London N7 9BH

Creative Director: Richard Dewing
Art Director: Paula Marchant
Designer: Isobel Gillan and Rod Teasdale
Senior Editor: Sally Green
Editor: Margaret Gilbey

Food Stylists: Eliza Baird and Emma Patmore
Photography: Ian Garlick and Howard Shooter

Typeset in Great Britain by
Central Southern Typesetters, Eastbourne

Manufactured in Hong Kong by
Regent Publishing Services Limited

Printed in China by
Leefung-Asco Printers Ltd.

**The publishers would like to thank Divertimenti of 139-141 Fulham Road, London SW3 6SB, England,
for the loan of a Pentole steamer. The full range of Pentole steamers is available from the store.**

CONTENTS

INTRODUCTION

Steaming, a cooking method thought to date back to before the discovery of fire, when foods were cooked over hot springs or stones, is now as popular as ever. Oriental cooking has always made great use of steaming as a main cooking method, both for health reasons and because ovens are very rare. Many foods are steamed, rather than baked, their main staple, rice, being perfect for this. The Chinese have used steamers for at least 3000 years or more, with early steamers being made in stoneware and originating in the province of Yunnan. From around the eighth century, thin cypress strips were used to make steamers and today they are constructed from bamboo with slatted bases. They may be stacked, usually up to three tiers, and placed over a wok containing boiling liquid. A tight-fitting bamboo lid seals in the steam.

Asian countries also steam a large proportion of their foods. The classic steamer used contains a chimney through the centre, which

distributes the steam among the tiers. A variation on the theme is found in Hawaii, where for many years the Kalua or traditional pig roast has been steamed in a pit in the ground. Stones and wood are used to create and retain the heat in the pit, which is covered with layers of leaves. The pig is then cooked in the steam and smoke.

So as you can see, steaming is no quirky fad, rather a tried and tested, versatile and rewarding method of cooking. Gone are its associations with stodgy, bland foods as the true versatility and richness of steaming is rediscovered. Healthier, more nutritious dishes may be simply produced by steaming; results are colourful, textured and flavourful.

Suitable for most foods and a surprising variety of recipes, steaming has great advantages over other cooking methods. A far higher level of nutrients, vitamins and minerals is retained than by any other cooking method. Steam cooking reduces vitamin C in vegetables by 40 per cent whereas boiling reduces it by 70 per cent because it is lost in the cooking water. Steaming does not immerse foods in water into which nutrients, particularly in vegetables, can escape. Foods are more nutritious generally when steamed, and as additional fat is not required for cooking it's also healthier and lower in fat. Even in recipes where higher fat content ingredients are called for, lower fat alternatives can generally be substituted, such as low-fat milk, cream and cheese, and poultry is always skinned to reduce fat content. Boiling does remain preferable for some vegetables such as mustard, turnip, collard greens or kale, which have a strong flavour, as this may be imparted to other foods during steaming.

Steaming is a moist cooking method, using the natural convection of heat that is travelling in air, steam or liquid. This gives tender results because foods are not exposed to intense, dry heat as with other cooking methods. Steaming protects foods, which during the

process are contained within sealed, perforated or slatted tiers, greaseproof paper or foil parcels or heatproof basins, and never come into contact with the heat source or steam-producing liquid. The tiers must sit at least 2.5 cm/1 inch above the liquid in order that it does not touch the food and overcook it on the base. Steam builds up inside the cooking vessels, produced from the heat of the liquid, cooking food in a really moist atmosphere.

Flavourings may be added to foods in a variety of ways. Either in the cooking liquid, which may be water flavoured with a stock cube or herbs and spices, fresh stock or wine, or by marinating foods before steaming. Spices such as ginger, chilli, cumin and coriander may be added to savoury recipes, and nutmeg, cinnamon, cloves and mint to sweet dishes. Herbs both fresh and dried, citrus juices, wines, spirits, oils, condiments and fruit juices may

also be used to make interesting and flavour-enhancing marinades for many foods before steaming. It is therefore always useful to have a selection of these to hand. As the flavours are kept within the cooking vessel, the resulting dishes are quite intense and enjoyable. Simple steaming suggestions include flavouring vegetables with a

squeeze of citrus juice or a sprinkling of chopped herbs, garlic or shallots, or else a drizzle of flavoured, good quality oil.

The three main methods of steaming

• The most popular and the quickest method for cooking meat, fish, vegetables, fruits and light desserts, is to suspend over boiling water, cover tightly and cook in the steam. This method may also be used for reheating and thawing foods.

• A longer method is cooking in a basin, bowl or paper or foil parcel over hot water. Foods are sealed within pleated greaseproof paper or foil and secured with string. This is done to allow for expansion as the steam fills the parcel or basin. The string secures the paper to the basin and gives a tight fit to prevent steam escaping. Food cooks in its own juices, since the boiling water and steam do not come into direct contact with it. This method gives an exact and even cooking temperature throughout the cooking time, which is why it is used for melting chocolate and for other tasks requiring consistent heat.

• In the Oriental method of steaming rice, which is used for dishes such as risotto and paella, the rice is immersed in water or stock, covered, and steamed until the liquid has been absorbed and the rice is cooked.

1

Water is added to the base of the saucepan.

2

For the longer method, foods are seated within pleated greaseproof paper.

3

Cover the steamer tightly with its lid.

4

The Oriental method of cooking rice is perfect for dishes such as risotto and paella.

TYPES OF STEAMERS

All steamers follow the same basic principle whereby foods are cooked in perforated or slatted tiers above a deep pan of hot liquid, covered with a tight-fitting lid. Steam produced by the hot liquid cooks the food in the tiers above without having direct contact with it. The liquid may be water, wine, stock or an accompanying sauce, any flavours that you wish to permeate the foods above. Use stock or salted water in the base of the steamer to simultaneously cook your pasta, rice or noodles to accompany a dish, but adjust cooking times to your preference for extra "bite".

There are three basic parts to a steamer: The first is a base compartment containing liquid which is heated to produce steam. The second is the steamer tier. The bottom is perforated so that steam can circulate around the food. There may be one or more of these, and if so the tiers stack on top of each other in order that different foods or courses may be steamed together without flavours combining. The third part of a steamer consists of a tight-fitting lid. This sits on top of either a single tier or the topmost tier and seals the whole unit, allowing steam to build up inside and cook the foods

Above left: *A good choice of electric steamers is now available.*

Above middle: *A stainless steel oven-top steamer. Several tiers may be acquired to make it even more versatile.*

Above right: *Chinese and bamboo steamers, which sit over a wok or saucepan, follow the same principle as other steamers.*

in a moist atmosphere. If the lid is not tight, cooking times will be a great deal longer and goodness will be lost during cooking. If using a pudding basin or dish to contain foods inside the tier, ensure that there is enough room to accommodate the juices that will build up during cooking.

Steaming is a radically different cooking method for some people and as such may require some adjusting to. To discover its true advantages takes time, but is well worth pursuing. Begin by using a simple and inexpensive expanding, perforated metal basket or platform placed over or inside a saucepan of hot liquid with a large roomy lid, large enough to allow steam to circulate around the food. A wok or Dutch oven will also work. This may be used to cook single layers of foods, although flavours cannot be separated, and is also good for reheating or thawing foods. However, the expanding basket takes up quite a lot of space in the pan and so is very limiting. A heatproof colander or two heatproof plates over a pan of boiling liquid are equally effective for this method of steaming.

A great advantage to the steaming method is that, since only one cooking pot is used for steaming, setting up and clearing up times are greatly reduced, as is washing up! No precooking is required and foods may be left to cook without being watched over and stirred, so leaving you free to relax. You may prefer an electric steamer to an oven-top,

which incorporates, among other things, a timer and thermostat for perfect and constant results. There is now a good selection of electric steamers available; virtually all of the major manufacturers of small kitchen appliances carry them in their product lines. They are quite large appliances which stand on the worktop, so keeping the stove free. They have the advantage of several stacking tiers so that complete meals may be cooked, and can generally take larger cuts of meat and whole poultry. A thermostatically controlled element in the base of the steamer heats the water or stock, and a timer switches the appliance off when cooking is complete. Specific rice steamers are often included, and drip trays that catch juices which can be used for making sauces and gravies.

In the 1950s, the High Rise Multi-Cooker, a low-tech steamer that could cook several different layers of food at one time, was introduced on one of television's first cooking shows. Since then models have greatly improved, and now steamers are made from stainless steel, the stovetop steamer being a common sight in the home. Several tiers may be acquired to make the standard steamer more versatile and as functional as an electric steamer, but only two to three levels is recommended.

Usually about 20 cm/8 inches in diameter, the stovetop steamer will amply hold a meal for the average family. A handle either side allows for easy lifting, and many have a thermocore base made from sandwiched aluminium and stainless steel to take up heat quickly and prevent hot spots, which can lead to burning. The disadvantages to these cookers over the electric steamers is that you cannot see inside the tiers during cooking, which means either opening the lid and losing some of the steam's efficiency, or relying solely on recommended cooking times. It is preferable to take the latter route and not to lift the lid during cooking. Oven-top steamers also of course use a ring on the cooker, which you may wish to free up for other, simultaneous cooking.

Chinese and bamboo steamers with slatted bases work on the same principle as all of the others. There are different sizes available, with two or three tiers topped with a solid lid. These sit over a wok, which usually contains either hot water or stock.

All of the recipes in the following chapters were tested in a stainless steel, stovetop, tiered steamer; cooking times are given as a guideline. Adjust times according to personal preference and to your model of steamer, following manufacturer's instructions. Bamboo, metal basket and colander steamers would produce approximately the same cooking times.

I have tried to bring you steaming at its best, using a wide variety of fresh, colourful and flavoursome ingredients in a great number of ways, both for your enjoyment and to demonstrate the versatility and full advantages of steaming. Most of us strive for healthy, tasty and easily prepared meals, and I guarantee that once you've dipped into this book and tried a few dishes, your diet will change for the better. Your cooking will be revolutionised.

Below: *The simple and inexpensive expanding metal basket is the best steamer with which to start.*

SOME GENERAL RULES

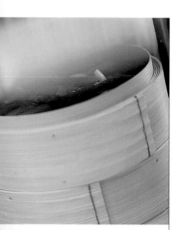

There are a few basic rules which should be followed when steaming to obtain perfect results every time:

• Ensure the ingredients used are of the best quality and in perfect condition. Choose lean meats which will be tender and not require lengthy cooking. Trim away excess fat before using and always cut across the grain for extra tenderness.

• Ensure the lid fits well to prevent the steam escaping and thus prolonging cooking time.

• When choosing fruit and vegetables, look for unblemished skins and good colour. Do not use "old" or bruised fruits, because steaming enhances flavours and aromas and any slight taint in a food will be accentuated.

• Make sure foods to be cooked together are of a similar or even size so that they will cook in the same amount of time. This applies to chopped foods and meat, fish or poultry portions.

• Do not allow the liquid in the base compartment to touch the food, or the food will boil and not steam. Suspend it at least 1 inch (2.5 cm) above the liquid.

• Liquid levels in the base of the steamer should be maintained for constant cooking, although it should never be more than two-thirds full. Top up with boiling liquid to maintain cooking.

• Cook food in a single layer or adjust cooking times accordingly as cooking will be slower.

• Arrange foods in the steamer compartment with space in between to allow steam to circulate and cook more efficiently. Always defrost frozen meats, fish and poultry before cooking, to allow for correct and complete cooking in the recommended times.

• Place meats, fish, poultry or juicy foods in the bottom tiers so that they cannot drip onto foods below.

• Allow an extra five minutes for foods cooked in upper tiers because they are further away from the steam.

• Finally, be sure to continue cooking foods that are not cooked through or not cooked to your liking, despite having been cooked for the recommended cooking time.

Most people think of boring, bland vegetables when they think of steaming, but you are about to discover that this could not be further from the truth.

The only real way to cook vegetables succesfully, for the best texture, colour, flavour and nutritional value, is steaming. Many imaginative dishes filled with the flavours from herbs, marinades and sauces follow in this chapter. There are main courses, accompaniments and snacks for all tastes and occasions— I promise, there's not a bland vegetable in sight.

VEGETABLES

Marinating the vegetables brings out their flavours without overpowering. This dish may be prepared in advance and stored in the refrigerator for up to 4 hours.

MIXED VEGETABLE PASTA

Serves 4

1 medium leek, halved and shredded

1 medium red pepper,
halved and thinly sliced

1 medium green pepper,
halved and thinly sliced

1 medium orange pepper,
halved and thinly sliced

8 baby corn, halved lengthwise

100 g/4 oz broccoli florets

50 g/2 oz broad beans

2 Tbsp stoned black olives, whole

150 ml/¼ pt dry white wine

3 garlic cloves, peeled and crushed

4 Tbsp olive oil

1 Tbsp walnut oil

3 Tbsp fresh mixed herbs, chopped

1 tsp dried chillies, chopped

250 g/8 oz spaghettini

❶ Place all of the prepared vegetables in a shallow glass dish. Mix the remaining ingredients together, except the spaghettini, and pour over the vegetables. Cover and leave to marinate for 2 hours, turning occasionally.

❷ Remove the vegetables and marinade from the dish and transfer to a greaseproof paper-lined steamer tier.

❸ Bring salted water to the boil in the base of the steamer and add the pasta. Place the vegetables over the top, cover with a tight-fitting lid and steam for 10 minutes or until the pasta and vegetables are cooked. Check the pasta before 10 minutes if you prefer a firmer texture.

❹ Drain the pasta and place in a warm serving bowl. Spoon the vegetables on top, season, and serve immediately.

If preferred, substitute dried beans, which have been soaked overnight and boiled rapidly for 10 minutes before use. This has to be done to remove toxins in the beans, which should be rinsed well before adding to the recipe.

MIXED BEANS WITH RICE

Serves 4

397 g/15 oz tin red kidney beans, drained
397 g/15 oz tin black eyed beans, drained
150 ml/¼ pt vegetable stock
2 Tbsp Worcestershire
or light soy sauce
2 Tbsp tomato purée
397 g/15 oz tin chopped tomatoes
Few drops Tabasco Sauce
1 medium red onion, cut into eight
2 celery sticks, thickly sliced
3 garlic cloves, peeled and crushed
1 medium green pepper, thinly sliced
225 g/8 oz sweet potato, cubed
100 g/4 oz tinned artichoke hearts, halved

For the rice
100 g/4 oz long-grain
and wild rice, mixed
200 ml/7 fl oz vegetable stock
225 g/8 oz spinach leaves, washed

❶ Put all the ingredients except the rice and stock in a deep bowl. Cover with pleated foil secured with string, and place in the steamer top.

❷ Bring the vegetable stock to the boil in the base of the steamer. Place the vegetables on top, cover, and steam for 25 minutes.

❸ Add the rice to the stock and cook for 15 minutes. Stir in the spinach and continue cooking for a further 3 to 5 minutes until the vegetables and rice are tender. Serve.

This is a pie with a difference; the crust consisting of a cheese-flavoured polenta batter is a wonderful topping for the colourful vegetable selection.

POLENTA PIE

Serves 4

½ small leek, shredded lengthwise
1 small carrot, cut into julienne strips
½ medium fennel bulb, thinly sliced
1 small red pepper, thinly sliced
½ small courgette, cut into julienne strips
1 small tomato, seeded and cut into strips
2 Tbsp stoned black olives, quartered
2 Tbsp olive oil
Juice and zest of 1 medium lemon
1 garlic clove, peeled and crushed
1 Tbsp fresh oregano, chopped
Freshly ground black pepper

For the batter
6 Tbsp plain flour
6 Tbsp polenta
1½ tsp baking powder
Pinch of salt
1 egg, beaten
150 ml/¼ pt milk
2 Tbsp freshly grated
Parmesan cheese
4 spring onions, finely chopped

❶ Put all of the prepared vegetables in a shallow glass dish. Mix the oil, lemon juice and zest, garlic, herbs and black pepper together, and pour over the vegetables, turning to coat. Cover and leave to marinate for 1 hour, turning occasionally.

❷ Sieve the flour into a mixing bowl and add the polenta, baking powder and salt. Mix the egg and milk together. Make a well in the centre of the dry mixture and gradually whisk in the egg and milk to make a smooth batter. Stir in the cheese and onions, and season well.

❸ Remove the vegetables from the marinade and spoon into the base of a lightly greased 1 litre/2 pint casserole dish. Pour the batter on top and cover in pleated foil secured with string.

❹ Place the basin in the top of the steamer, cover, and steam for 50 minutes until the batter is set. Serve immediately with potatoes or rice and a green salad.

This is a filling dish which may be made with a variety of nuts for an equally good result. Try pecans or walnuts as an alternative. If possible, allow the loaf to stand for 10 minutes before slicing.

CASHEW AND ASPARAGUS BOMBE

Serves 4

1 Tbsp olive oil

1 medium red onion, chopped

2 garlic cloves, peeled and crushed

175 g/6 oz unsalted cashews, finely chopped

6 Tbsp wholemeal breadcrumbs

1 egg, beaten

1 large potato, peeled, cooked and mashed

2 Tbsp fresh mixed herbs, chopped

1 tsp yeast extract

150 ml/¼ pt vegetable stock

150 g/5 oz asparagus spears

For the sauce

150 ml/¼ pt vegetable stock

1 Tbsp tomato purée

3 Tbsp dry sherry

2 Tbsp butter

❶ Heat the oil in a pan and sauté the onion and garlic for 2 to 3 minutes until beginning to soften. Add the nuts and breadcrumbs.

❷ Remove from the heat and stir in the egg, potato, herbs, yeast extract and stock. Mix well and press half the mixture into the base of a 900 ml/1½ pint pudding dish or mould lined with greaseproof paper, which fits into the steamer tier.

❸ Arrange the asparagus spears on top and spoon on remaining cashew mixture. Cover with pleated greaseproof paper and secure with string.

❹ Steam the loaf in the top of a steamer for 1 hour or until set. Leave to stand for 10 minutes before turning out and slicing.

❺ Meanwhile, heat the stock, tomato purée and sherry for the sauce, and bring to the boil. Gradually whisk in the butter and serve with the sliced loaf.

These mushrooms hint of Mexican cuisine and are surprisingly simple to prepare. They make an ideal lunch with salad, soured cream and fresh bread.

STUFFED MUSHROOMS

Serves 4

8 large open-cap mushrooms,
   peeled and cleaned
4 Tbsp wholemeal breadcrumbs
4 spring onions, chopped
1 ripe avocado, finely chopped
1 small red chilli, sliced
1 large tomato, seeded and chopped
2 tsp lemon juice
4 Tbsp freshly grated mozzarella cheese
1 Tbsp fresh coriander, chopped

1 Remove the stalks from the mushrooms and chop the stalks finely. Stir into the breadcrumbs, spring onions, avocado, chilli, tomato and lemon juice, mixing well.

2 Spoon the mixture onto the mushroom caps, piling up, pressing and shaping with a spoon, so the mounds hold together. Sprinkle the cheese on top, then the coriander.

3 Place the mushroom caps in the steamer top, cover with the lid, and steam for 10 minutes until tender. Serve with salad.

This dish is full of Mediterranean flavours and makes a great snack or side dish. Marrow could be used in place of the courgettes. This dish is also ideal cold with meats or fish, as a salad. When young, the whole aubergine is tender and wonderfully edible; older aubergines should be peeled. Overripe aubergine can also be salted heavily and left to drain 20 minutes, to reduce the fruit's bitterness (aubergine is technically a berry).

GARLIC, COURGETTE AND AUBERGINE

Serves 4

450 g/1 lb courgettes
2 large aubergines, halved and thickly sliced
2 medium leeks, thickly sliced
4 garlic cloves, peeled and crushed
397 g/15 oz tin artichoke hearts,
   drained and halved
4 Tbsp olive oil
Freshly ground black pepper
1 Tbsp fresh mixed herbs, chopped

1 Salt the aubergine if desired. Mix together the aubergines, courgettes, leeks, garlic, artichoke hearts, oil, black pepper and herbs. Stir well and transfer to a foil-lined steamer tier.

2 Cover with a tight-fitting lid and steam for 45 minutes or until the vegetables are tender. Serve with steamed rice or as an accompaniment to plain meats.

Red split lentils are a great staple ingredient to keep on hand, as they require no presoaking and add great flavour, fibre and many essential nutrients including calcium, vitamins A and D, iron and phosphorus.

LENTIL PILAU

Serves 4

1 Tbsp oil
4 spring onions, finely chopped
175 g/6 oz dry red lentils
250 g/8 oz basmati rice
1 tsp turmeric
1 medium carrot, grated
1 medium red pepper, finely diced
2 Tbsp sultanas
25 g/1 oz French beans,
finely chopped
1 celery stick, finely diced
1 tsp chilli powder
1 tsp fennel seeds
1 tsp ground cumin
1 Tbsp fresh coriander, chopped
600 ml/1 pt vegetable stock

For the sauce
600 ml/1 pt passata
1 medium onion, finely chopped
2 garlic cloves, peeled and crushed
1 Tbsp fresh coriander, chopped
Salt and freshly ground black pepper

❶ Place all of the pilau ingredients in the base of the steamer, cover, and cook for 30 minutes until the stock has been absorbed.

❷ Spoon the mixture into ramekins or moulds, and place in a steamer tier.

❸ Wash out the base of the steamer and put in all of the sauce ingredients. Stack the tier with the pilau moulds on top and cover with a tight-fitting lid.

❹ Bring the sauce to the boil, reduce the heat slightly, and cook for 10 minutes.

❺ Turn the rice moulds out onto warm serving plates and spoon the sauce around the base. Garnish with coriander and serve.

A favourite Mexican dish, these irresistible tortillas are a great informal supper dish. Use any good combination of vegetables that you have in your store cupboard.

SPICY VEGETABLES WITH TORTILLAS

Serves 4

1 medium onion, quartered and thinly sliced

4 baby corn, halved lengthwise

2 celery sticks, cut into julienne strips

1 medium courgette, cut into julienne strips
  or thinly sliced

4 Tbsp mangetout, sliced

1 medium red pepper, cut into strips

2 large tomatoes, seeded and cubed

1 medium green chilli, thinly sliced

1 garlic clove, peeled and crushed

2 Tbsp tomato purée

150 ml/¼ pt vegetable stock

2 Tbsp fresh coriander, chopped

1 tsp ground coriander

8 flour tortillas, frozen or fresh

150 ml/¼ pt plain yoghurt

❶ Mix all of the vegetables together in a heatproof bowl and place in the top of the steamer.

❷ Mix the tomato purée, stock, 1 tablespoon chopped coriander and ground coriander together, and pour over the vegetables in the bowl. Cover with pleated greaseproof paper and steam for 15 minutes until the vegetables are tender.

❸ Lay the tortillas in the base of the second tier of the steamer and place over the vegetables for the last 5 minutes of cooking time or until warmed through.

❹ Mix the yoghurt and remaining fresh coriander in a serving bowl.

❺ Spoon the vegetable mixture into the tortillas and serve with yoghurt.

Hot salads are a delicious alternative and can be served as a meal with hot crusty bread or as a side dish. Be sure to serve it immediately because the chicory browns very quickly.

STEAMED CHICORY SALAD

Serves 4

4 large heads chicory
1 medium carrot, cut into julienne strips
3 spring onions, shredded
2.5 cm/1 inch piece fresh ginger, shredded
2 Tbsp pine kernels
2 Tbsp freshly grated Parmesan cheese
Freshly ground black pepper

For the dressing
3 Tbsp walnut oil
2 Tbsp lemon juice
1 Tbsp clear honey
2 Tbsp fresh mixed herbs, chopped
1 Tbsp balsamic vinegar

❶ Separate the chicory heads into individual leaves, rinse and dry, and arrange in the centre of four large squares of greaseproof paper.

❷ Add the carrot, spring onions, ginger and pine kernels.

❸ Mix the dressing ingredients, shaking well. Bring the sides of each greaseproof square up to make a parcel and pour ¼ of the dressing into each parcel. Seal and place in the top of the steamer.

❹ Steam for 10 minutes until hot. Open the parcels and sprinkle the cheese over the top. Season and serve immediately with hot bread.

This is a really simple side dish which is great with poultry or fish. Cucumber and peas or other varieties of bean will work equally well.

COURGETTE AND BEANS WITH GARLIC AND MINT

Serves 4

2 large courgettes, thickly sliced
100 g/4 oz green beans, thickly sliced
2 tsp lemon juice
1 Tbsp fresh mint, chopped
2 garlic cloves, peeled and crushed
2 Tbsp butter
Salt and freshly ground black pepper
Fresh mint sprigs and lemon zest, to garnish

❶ Cut a large square of foil and place the vegetables in the centre. Fold up sides, without closing, to a size that will fit in your steamer.

❷ Top the vegetables with the lemon juice, mint, garlic, butter and seasoning, and close the foil around the vegetables to form a parcel, sealing well.

❸ Place the parcel in the steamer tier over boiling water. Cover with a tight-fitting lid and steam for 8 to 10 minutes until the vegetables are tender. Garnish and serve.

Goat's cheese gives a strong and distinctive flavour to peppers, and is steamed until just melted to perfection. Serve with a green salad for a very colourful dish.

GOAT'S CHEESE-FILLED PEPPERS

Serves 4

2 medium red peppers
2 medium yellow peppers

For the filling
350 g/12 oz goat's cheese
2 Tbsp pine kernels
2 garlic cloves, peeled and crushed
2 Tbsp pimento-stuffed green olives, chopped
2 celery sticks, thinly sliced
2 Tbsp fresh parsley, chopped
2 Tbsp raisins

❶ Bring water to the boil in the base of the steamer. Cut each of the peppers in half lengthwise and remove the core and seeds. Blanch the peppers for a scant 5 minutes in the water and then remove with a slotted spoon.

❷ Mix the remaining ingredients together and spoon into the pepper shells. Place in the base of the steamer top over the boiling water. Cover tightly and steam for 20 minutes. Serve with a crisp green salad.

You may use fresh artichokes in this recipe if preferred but, for speed and ease, tinned artichoke hearts are just as delicious. This is an ideal side dish for grilled or steamed chicken.

MEDITERRANEAN ARTICHOKES

Serves 4

397 g/14 oz tin artichoke hearts, drained
3 garlic cloves, peeled and crushed
1 large onion, cut into 16
1 Tbsp butter
2 Tbsp Madeira
250 g/8 oz chopped fresh or tinned tomatoes
1 Tbsp tomato purée
1 tsp brown sugar
2 Tbsp fresh basil
or marjoram, chopped
2 Tbsp black stoned olives, halved

❶ Cut the artichoke hearts into halves.

❷ Place all of the ingredients in a heatproof dish which fits a steamer tier. Cover snugly with pleated foil and with a tight-fitting lid.

❸ Steam for 20 minutes or until the vegetables are tender. Serve immediately.

Individual timbales are ideal as a dinner party starter. Be sure to press any excess moisture from the spinach before combining with the eggs, otherwise the resulting dish will be very watery.

ASPARAGUS TIMBALE

Serves 4

225 g/8 oz asparagus tips

1 small leek, thinly sliced

225 g/8 oz spinach leaves, washed

1 large opencap mushroom, peeled, cleaned and chopped

2 garlic cloves, peeled and crushed

1 Tbsp fresh thyme, chopped

6 eggs, beaten

2 Tbsp freshly grated Parmesan cheese

Salt and freshly ground black pepper

Asparagus spears and grated Parmesan cheese, to garnish

❶ Place the vegetables, garlic and thyme in the base of a steamer tier over boiling water. Cover and steam for 10 minutes.

❷ Transfer the vegetables to a food processor or blender and purée for 30 seconds until smooth. Beat in the eggs and cheese. Season well.

❸ Spoon the mixture into four ramekins, cover each with pleated greaseproof paper, secured with string. Place the dishes in the top of the steamer and cook over boiling water for 40 minutes until set. Garnish with asparagus spears, blanched until tender, and Parmesan cheese. Serve with hot toasted bread according to taste.

These stuffed aubergines can be served as a main meal or as a starter, if the recipe is halved in quantity. Tahini dip is available from good healthfood shops and makes an ideal accompaniment.

MIDDLE EASTERN AUBERGINES

Serves 4

4 small aubergines
4 Tbsp couscous
1 garlic clove, peeled and crushed
2 tsp light brown sugar
1 medium tomato, roughly chopped
50 g/2 oz dried apricots, finely chopped
25 g/1 oz blanched almonds, chopped
2 Tbsp fresh coriander, chopped
2 spring onions, finely chopped
1 tsp ground coriander
Salt and freshly ground black pepper
Tahini dip, to serve

❶ Cut the aubergines in half lengthwise and sprinkle liberally with salt. Leave to stand in a sieve, flesh down, for 20 minutes, then rinse under cold water. Pat dry.

❷ Meanwhile, soak the couscous in boiling water for 20 minutes. Drain off any excess liquid.

❸ Scoop the flesh out of the aubergines, leaving a thin lining in the skin. Chop the flesh coarsely and mix with the couscous, garlic, sugar, tomato, apricots, almonds, fresh coriander, spring onions and ground coriander. Season well.

❹ Spoon the mixture into the aubergine shells and place in the steamer tiers. Cover with a tight-fitting lid and steam for 15 to 20 minutes. Serve hot with tahini dip and salad.

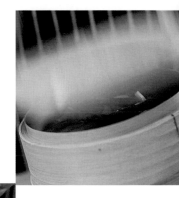

Fresh baby vegetables have a flavour all their own. In this dish they are served simply, with a yoghurt and garlic sauce and plain pasta. Use any combination of mixed vegetables that you have to hand for a spur-of-the-moment dish.

FETTUCCINE PRIMAVERA

Serves 4

300 g/10 oz fettuccine

75 g/3 oz broccoli florets

4 baby carrots, halved lengthwise

1 medium red pepper, cubed

1 medium green pepper, cubed

1 medium red onion, quartered and
   thinly sliced

50 g/2 oz broad beans

25 g/1 oz peas

2 garlic cloves, peeled and crushed

6 Tbsp freshly grated
Cheddar cheese

5 Tbsp plain yoghurt

Pinch of cayenne pepper

Salt and freshly ground black pepper

❶ Bring a large quantity of salted water to the boil in the base of the steamer and add the pasta.

❷ Place all of the vegetables in a greaseproof paper-lined steamer tier, cover with a tight-fitting lid, and steam over the pasta for 10 minutes. Check the pasta before 10 minutes to ensure it does not overcook.

❸ Add the cheese, yoghurt and cayenne pepper to the vegetables and keep warm.

❹ Drain the pasta and transfer to a warm serving dish. Top with the vegetables, season well, and serve immediately.

Poppy seeds give a great flavour to these glazed vegetables, but other seeds such as fennel may be used to vary the taste. A perfect accompaniment to marinated lamb or pork.

HONEY-GLAZED VEGETABLES

Serves 4

2 medium baby turnips, trimmed and halved

2 medium carrots, cut into julienne strips

2 celery sticks, cut into julienne strips

1 large courgette, cut into julienne strips or sliced thinly

4 baby corn, halved lengthwise

3 Tbsp clear honey

2 Tbsp vegetable stock

2 tsp light soy sauce

2 tsp poppy seeds

Salt and freshly ground black pepper

❶ Place all of the vegetables in a shallow dish. Mix the honey, stock and soy sauce, and pour over the vegetables.

❷ Sprinkle the poppy seeds over the vegetables, turning them to coat well.

❸ Place the vegetables in a greaseproof paper-lined steamer tier and cover with a tight-fitting lid.

❹ Steam for 20 minutes or until the vegetables are tender. Season with salt and freshly ground black pepper.

Beetroot is a very nutritious but often neglected vegetable. Choose small to medium beetroots as these will be more tender. Remove the leaves (also edible and very nutritious) as soon as you get home, as the leaves leach nutrients from the beetroot. Leave on about 2.5 cm/1 inch of stem; this helps retain the nutrients while cooking. Peel after cooking. This dish is packed with colour and flavour, and should be served as a side dish with a milder entrée or as a starter with a crisp green salad. It may be made in advance and left to chill in the refrigerator until required (up to 4 hours). Peaches or nectarines can be used in place of the apricots.

SPICY BABY BEETROOTS AND ORANGE

Serves 4

10 small beetroots, gently washed

150 ml/¼ pt orange juice

150 ml/¼ pt red wine

2 Tbsp garlic vinegar

2 tsp clear honey

2 spring onions, thickly sliced

Orange zest and segments, to garnish

❶ Place the beetroots in the steamer, cover with a tight-fitting lid, and steam over the orange juice, wine, vinegar, honey and spring onions for 15 to 20 minutes until the beetroots are fork-tender.

❷ Remove the beetroots, and set aside. Bring the liquid to the boil until thickened. Meanwhile, peel the beetroots and slice into rounds.

❸ Arrange the beetroots on warm serving plates and spoon the sauce over the top. Garnish and serve immediately.

New potatoes are just young potatoes, of any variety. Choose firm, well-shaped and blemish-free potatoes of roughly equal size, so that they all cook in the same amount of time.

GARLIC NEW POTATOES

Serves 4

450 g/1 lb new potatoes, lightly scrubbed
2 Tbsp olive oil
2 garlic cloves, peeled and crushed
1 Tbsp fresh basil, chopped

For the sauce
1 small onion, quartered and thinly sliced
1 tsp paprika
Pinch of cayenne pepper
1 tsp fennel seeds
300 ml/½ pt passata
300 ml/½ pt vegetable stock
2 Tbsp fresh basil, chopped
1 tsp brown sugar
Fresh basil, to garnish

❶ Line a steamer tier with foil, making an edge to form a dish. Put the potatoes, oil, garlic and basil in the foil.

❷ Place the sauce ingredients in the base of the steamer and bring to the boil. Cook the potatoes, covered, over the sauce for 45 minutes until the potatoes are tender. Garnish with basil, and serve with the sauce.

Peppers have their own special flavour, especially when marinated and steamed in this lovely combination of ingredients. They may be served over steamed rice if preferred to noodles.

CHILLI-MARINATED PEPPERS OVER NOODLES

Serves 4

1 large green pepper

1 large red pepper

1 large yellow pepper

1 large orange pepper

1 medium red chilli

2 garlic cloves, peeled and crushed

2 Tbsp soy sauce

2 Tbsp clear honey

1 Tbsp dry sherry

Juice of 1 medium lime

1 Tbsp fresh rosemary

Freshly ground black pepper

1 ½ pt vegetable stock

250 g/8 oz egg noodles

❶ Remove the seeds from the peppers and cut into cubes. Place in a shallow glass dish which fits the steamer, with the remaining ingredients except the noodles, cover, and leave to marinate for 1 hour, turning occasionally.

❷ Transfer the dish to the steamer, cover with a tight-fitting lid, and cook over boiling stock for 15 minutes.

❸ Add the noodles to the stock in the base of the steamer. Cook a further 5 minutes until the peppers are tender. Drain the noodles and place in a warmed serving bowl. Spoon the peppers on top and serve immediately.

Fish and seafood are among the best sources of protein available to us, and are low in fats. The fats found in fish are polyunsaturated and therefore healthier than animal fats.

There are so many varieties of fish and shellfish to choose from, the world really is "your oyster" when choosing delicious recipes to cook. Having a wide range of textures, colours and flavours, these foods are simple to prepare and quickly cooked, making for many speedy and enjoyable meals.

Steaming is the ideal method of cooking for fish and shellfish. A moist method which requires no additional fat, it seals in all of the goodness to give us fish at its best.

In this chapter I have tried to use a wide choice of fish and shellfish, but most recipes are interchangeable to accommodate your favourites. There are simple suppers, light lunches, and special dishes for those more important occasions. I'm sure you will agree that steamed fish is just superb.

FISH & SHELLFISH

The bacon and orange in this stuffing are perfect partners to the wonderful full flavour of steamed trout. Citrus fruits are an ideal accompaniment for oily fish. Grapefruit could also be used.

COUSCOUS-STUFFED TROUT

Serves 4

4 whole trout (about 225 g/8 oz each),
   cleaned
1 large Cos lettuce, washed and separated

For the stuffing
100 g/4 oz couscous
2 Tbsp butter
1 Tbsp olive oil
2 rashers smoked bacon, finely chopped
1 small leek, finely chopped
50 g/2 oz mushrooms, cleaned and
   finely chopped
1 small orange, peeled, segmented
   and chopped
2 Tbsp pine kernels
2 Tbsp fresh coriander, chopped

1 Wash the trout inside and out, under cold running water. Pat dry with kitchen paper and set aside.

2 Soak the couscous in boiling water for 10 minutes until swollen. Drain and transfer to a lined steamer top, cover with a tight-fitting lid and steam over hot water for 15 minutes until softened. Stir in half the butter.

3 Meanwhile, heat the olive oil with the remaining butter in a frying pan and sauté the bacon and leek for 5 minutes. Add the mushrooms and cook for a further 2 minutes.

4 Spoon the mixture into the couscous together with the orange, pine kernels and coriander. Mix thoroughly.

5 Using a spoon, stuff the cavity of each trout with a quarter of the stuffing, pressing it in with the back of the spoon.

6 Steam the lettuce leaves for 1 minute until pliable. Use the lettuce to wrap around each trout, leaving the tail visible.

7 Put the fish in a steamer top, cover tightly and cook for 20 to 25 minutes or until thoroughly cooked. Chop off heads and tails to suit taste. Serve with a lemon or garlic mayonnaise.

This recipe is also delicious using meaty white fish or rolls of smoked salmon in place of the salmon fillet. Thread chunky vegetables between the fish, such as courgettes, small tomatoes and onions for variety.

SALMON AND WILD MUSHROOM KEBABS

Serves 4

1 kg/2 lb salmon fillet or steaks, skinned

8 wild mushrooms, cleaned

1 small yellow pepper, cubed

Salt and freshly ground black pepper

Juice and zest of 1 medium lime

1 garlic clove, peeled and crushed

1 Tbsp garlic wine vinegar

2 Tbsp olive oil

1 tsp prepared Dijon mustard

1 Tbsp fresh dill, chopped

150 ml/¼ pt fish stock

Lime wedges and fresh dill, to garnish

Green salad, to serve

1 Wash the fish under running water and pat dry. Cut into cubes, removing any bones if using steaks. Halve the mushrooms and transfer to a shallow glass dish with the fish and yellow pepper. Season well.

2 Mix the lime juice and zest, garlic, vinegar, olive oil, mustard and dill. Pour into the glass dish to coat the ingredients well. Cover and marinate for 2 hours, turning occasionally.

3 Cut four wooden kebab skewers in half. Thread on the fish, pepper and mushrooms, alternating ingredients. Reserve marinade.

4 Bring the water in the base of the steamer to the boil. Lay a sheet of foil in the base of the top of the steamer and arrange kebabs inside. Cover with a tight-fitting lid and reduce heat slightly. Cook for 15 minutes.

5 Meanwhile, bring the marinade and stock to the boil in a saucepan until reduced by half. Arrange kebabs on a serving plate and pour the hot marinade over top. Garnish with lime wedges and dill, and serve.

Steaming this delicious pasta sauce retains all of the wonderful colours, textures and flavours of the fish and vegetable for a perfect supper dish. Use trout fillets in place of salmon if preferred.

SALMON AND BROCCOLI PENNE

Serves 4

350 g/12 oz dry penne

250 g/8 oz broccoli florets

1/2 Tbsp olive oil

1 tsp garlic wine vinegar

2 garlic cloves, peeled and crushed

Juice and zest of 1 medium orange

350 g/12 oz salmon fillet, skinned and
    cut into cubes

6 Tbsp dry white wine

150 ml/¼ pt single cream

2 Tbsp fresh dill, chopped

2 Tbsp freshly grated Parmesan cheese

Salt and freshly ground black pepper

Orange wedges and dill, to garnish

❶ Half fill the steamer base with water and bring to the boil. Add the pasta and season with a little salt (add it later for "al dente,").

❷ Place the broccoli in a greaseproof paper-lined steamer tier. Mix the oil, vinegar, garlic, and orange juice and rind together and pour over the broccoli. Rinse the salmon under running water and pat dry. Add the salmon to the pan and cover with a tight-fitting lid.

❸ Set on top of the pasta in salted boiling water for 10 minutes or until the pasta and fish are cooked through.

❹ Meanwhile, heat the wine, cream, dill and Parmesan in a saucepan to just below boiling point. Season to taste.

❺ Drain the pasta and transfer to a warmed serving dish. Spoon the fish and broccoli on top and spoon the sauce over. Garnish, and serve immediately.

This easy pesto sauce is a terrific partner to salmon, complementing the fish's flavour and colour. The sauce may be made 24 hours in advance and stored in the refrigerator.

QUICK FISH WITH PESTO

Serves 4

For the pesto

3 garlic cloves, peeled and chopped

2 Tbsp pine kernels

1 large bunch basil, rinsed

5 Tbsp freshly grated Parmesan cheese

300 ml/½ pt Extra virgin olive oil

2 Tbsp lemon juice

225 g/8 oz dry fusilli

8 salmon trout fillets (about 75 g/3 oz each),
    skinned

Salt and freshly ground black pepper

❶ Put the garlic, pine kernels, basil and Parmesan cheese in a food processor. Gradually blend in the oil with the machine running. Stir in the lemon juice once the sauce is blended.

❷ Meanwhile, bring the water to the boil in the base of the steamer, season with salt and add the pasta. Rinse the fish under cold running water and pat dry. Put the fish fillets in a greaseproof paper-lined steamer top, season with salt and black pepper, cover, and steam for 10 minutes or until the fish is cooked.

❸ Remove the fish and arrange on four serving plates. Spoon the pesto onto the fish and serve with the drained pasta. Garnish with basil.

The colourful relish which accompanies this fish can be stored in the refrigerator; should you have any left over, serve chilled with other fish or meat such as plain pork or chicken.

SALMON WITH CORN RELISH

Serves 4

900 g/2 lb salmon fillet, cut into 4 equal
  pieces
2 sprigs fresh rosemary
1 garlic clove, peeled
Freshly ground black pepper

For the relish
2 corn on the cob
300 ml/½ pt fish stock
1 small red pepper, seeded and finely
  chopped
1 small green chilli, chopped
2 spring onions, chopped
1 Tbsp garlic wine vinegar
1 Tbsp olive oil
2 tsp light brown sugar

❶ Wash the fish under running water and pat dry. Arrange with the rosemary and garlic on a sheet of dampened greaseproof paper in the base of the steamer top. Season with pepper.

❷ Put the corn cobs, stock, red pepper and chilli in the base of the steamer and bring to the boil.

❸ Put the fish tier on top, cover with a tight-fitting lid and cook for 15 to 20 minutes. Remove the fish and keep warm, discarding the rosemary and garlic.

❹ Remove the corn, red pepper and chilli from the stock. Cut the kernels from the corn cobs and transfer to a bowl with the chilli and red pepper, spring onions, vinegar, oil and sugar.

❺ Boil the stock rapidly to reduce by half and add to the corn mixture.

❻ Arrange the fish on a warmed serving plate. Garnish with the relish, and serve.

These colourful fish twists are perfect for a dinner party or when you want to impress, without spending hours in the kitchen. They are also a delightful alternative to crab sticks. Plaice is a very versatile, low-fat mild fish.
For a low-fat version of the sauce, blend 8 tablespoons plain yoghurt with 1 teaspoon each lime and lemon juice and 1 peeled and crushed garlic clove.

FISH TWISTS WITH LIME SAUCE

Serves 4

650 g/1½ lb salmon trout fillets, skinned
450 g/1 lb plaice fillets, skinned
Juice and zest of 1 medium lime
1 garlic clove, peeled and crushed

For the sauce
250 g/8 oz butter
3 egg yolks
2 Tbsp lime juice
Zest of 1 medium lime
7 garlic cloves, peeled and crushed
2 Tbsp fresh parsley, chopped
Lime wedges and dill, to garnish

❶ Rinse the fillets under running water and pat dry. Cut the salmon trout into eight strips and the plaice into four. Trim fish fillets into identical lengths. On a chopping board twist two salmon trout fillets around one plaice fillet.

❷ Line a steamer tier with greaseproof paper and place the fish twists in the steamer tier with the lime and garlic.

❸ Cover with a tight-fitting lid and steam over boiling water for 10 minutes or until the fish is cooked through.

❹ After 5 minutes cooking time, begin to make the sauce. Melt the butter in a saucepan. Blend the egg yolks with the lime juice and zest in a food processor and gradually pour in the melted butter with the food processor running. Stir in the garlic and parsley and transfer the sauce to a mixing bowl.

❺ Stand the bowl over a saucepan of hot water while transferring the cooked fish onto warmed plates. Spoon the sauce around the fish, and garnish with lime wedges and dill. Serve immediately.

Marinating the fish in orange, ginger and onion gives it a delicious flavour and keeps it lovely and moist. A colourful and flavourful feast, it may be made with any white fish. A small grapefruit may be used in place of the orange, using only the flesh and not the zest.

ORANGE-GINGER MARINATED WHITEFISH

Serves 4

4 large whitefish fillets, skinned
  (about 175 g/6 oz each)
Juice and zest of ½ medium orange
2.5 cm/½ inch piece fresh ginger, grated
2 garlic cloves, crushed
4 spring onions, shredded
1 medium orange, segmented
4 Tbsp dry white wine
2 Tbsp butter
1 Tbsp fresh chives, chopped

1 Rinse the fish under running water and pat dry. Place in a shallow glass dish. Mix half of the orange juice and zest, the ginger, garlic, spring onions and half of the orange segments in the dish. Cover and marinate for 1 hour, turning occasionally.

2 Remove the fish, orange and spring onions from the dish, reserving the marinade, and place in a greaseproof paper-lined steamer tier. Cover with a tight-fitting lid and steam for 10 to 15 minutes.

3 Meanwhile, pour the marinade into a small saucepan with the remaining orange juice, zest and the wine. Bring to the boil and boil rapidly for 2 to 3 minutes to reduce. Remove from the heat. Stir in the butter to give a glossy sauce and add the chives.

4 Serve the fish on warm plates with the sauce. Garnish with fresh chives and orange segments and serve with freshly steamed rice.

This dish has a Mediterranean flavour, using fresh ripe tomatoes, olives and citrus juice. Served on a croûte of focaccia, it is ideal with a crisp white wine.

COD FOCACCIA

Serves 4

4 cod fillets, skinned
  (about 100 g/4 oz each)
3 Tbsp olive oil
Juice and zest of 2 medium limes
3 garlic cloves, peeled and crushed
1 tsp ground coriander
1 tsp fennel seeds
2 large tomatoes, seeded and cut into eight
4 Tbsp stoned black olives, whole

For the croûte
3 Tbsp butter
1 Tbsp olive oil
4 thick slices focaccia

❶ Wash the fish under running water and pat dry. Place in a shallow glass dish. Mix the oil, lime, garlic, coriander and fennel seeds and pour over the fish, turning to coat well. Cover and leave to marinate for at least 1 hour, turning occasionally.

❷ Remove the fish from the dish, reserving the marinade, and place in a greaseproof paper-lined steamer tier with the tomatoes and olives. Cover with a tight-fitting lid and steam for 10 to 15 minutes or until the fish is cooked through.

❸ Meanwhile, melt the butter with the oil in a frying pan. Fry the focaccia in the butter and oil for 2 minutes, turn over, and cook for 2 minutes. Drain on kitchen paper. Transfer the marinade to a small saucepan and heat through until hot.

❹ Top each focaccia with a piece of fish, tomatoes and olives, pour the warm marinade over, and serve with a green salad.

This dish is quite spicy, but the heat can easily be reduced by halving the quantity of chilli. The peppers may be prepared up to 24 hours in advance and stored in the refrigerator.

WHITEFISH IN A SPICY PEPPER SAUCE

Serves 4

8 white fish fillets (about 75 g/3 oz each),
   skinned
1 Tbsp olive oil
Juice of ½ medium lemon
4 spring onions, chopped
2 sprigs fresh basil
Salt and freshly ground black pepper

For the sauce
2 large red peppers
1 medium red chilli
300 ml/½ pt fish stock
2 Tbsp fresh basil, chopped
Fresh basil leaves, to garnish

1 Wash the fish under running water and pat dry. Place in a shallow glass dish. Mix the oil, lemon, spring onions and basil sprigs, season and pour over the fish. Cover and leave for 2 hours, turning occasionally.

2 Halve the red peppers, removing seeds. Place under a hot grill, skin side uppermost, for 10 minutes. Transfer to a plastic bag, seal and leave for 10 minutes. Remove from the bag and peel.

3 Finely chop the peppers and chilli and put in the base of the steamer with the fish stock and chopped basil. Lay a sheet of foil in the steamer top and place the fish fillets and marinade inside. Cover with a tight-fitting lid and steam for 10 minutes over the sauce ingredients.

4 Remove the fish and spring onions from the steamer and keep warm. Transfer the red peppers and stock to a blender and blend until smooth. Arrange the fish fillets on warmed serving plates. Garnish with the sauce and fresh basil leaves, and serve.

These individual pots may be made with any smoked fish such as cod or salmon for variation. Creamed cottage cheese is used in the recipe, but sieved small-curd cottage cheese will work equally well.

SMOKED HADDOCK POTS

Serves 4

450 g/1 lb fresh spinach, washed and
   stems removed

225 g/8 oz smoked haddock fillets, skinned
   and flaked

1 egg

1 egg yolk

150 g/5 oz creamed cottage cheese

8 Tbsp plain yoghurt

2 Tbsp fresh parsley, chopped

Juice and zest of 1 medium lime

Freshly ground black pepper

1 large tomato, thinly sliced

Lime slices and tomato, to garnish

❶ Prepare the steamer, bringing the water to the boil. Steam the spinach in the top of the steamer for 2 minutes. Remove, and squeeze out any moisture.

❷ Rinse the fish under running water and pat dry. Place with the egg, egg yolk, cheese, yoghurt, parsley, lime juice, and zest and pepper in a food processor and blend for 30 seconds.

❸ Arrange half of the spinach in the base of four lightly buttered ramekins and top with half of the fish mixture.

❹ Layer the tomatoes on top, and then the remaining fish mixture. Top with the remaining spinach.

❺ Place the dishes in the top of the steamer, cover with a tight-fitting lid and steam for 20 minutes until set. Invert the ramekins onto serving plates, garnish and serve with hot or toasted bread.

Skate is a wonderful-looking and tasting fish, but if unavailable, use meaty cod or monkfish in its place. Tarragon and fish are a perfect combination, but dill or fennel tops may be used instead for an equally good sauce.

SKATE WITH TARRAGON BUTTER

Serves 4

2 medium-sized skate wings,
   about 900 g/2 lb
150 ml/¼ pt dry vermouth
Juice and zest of 1 medium orange
1 small leek, medium sliced
1 medium red onion, quartered and
   thinly sliced

For the tarragon butter
100 g/4 oz butter
2 Tbsp fresh tarragon, chopped
Few drops of Tabasco Sauce
2 tsp mixed peppercorns, partly crushed
Salt
Tarragon sprigs, to garnish

❶ Rinse the skate under cold water and pat dry with kitchen paper. Cut the skate wings in half to give four equal portions.

❷ Line two steamer tiers with greaseproof paper and place two portions of fish in each.

❸ Mix the vermouth, half of the orange juice and zest and pour over the fish. Add half of the leek and onion to each tier and stack on top of each other in the steamer base. Cover with a tight-fitting lid and cook for 20 minutes, swapping the tiers over halfway through cooking, until the fish is cooked through.

❹ Meanwhile, melt the butter in a small saucepan and add the remaining orange juice and zest. Stir in the remaining sauce ingredients and heat gently for 2 to 3 minutes.

❺ Remove the skate from the steamer and transfer to warmed serving plates. Spoon the butter over the skate, garnish with orange slices and fresh tarragon sprigs, and serve with freshly steamed vegetables including new potatoes.

Crêpes are a great way to serve fish for a light meal. Make the crêpes up to 24 hours in advance and warm them in the top of the steamer for a few minutes before filling. Crêpes may also be cooked and frozen. Simply defrost at room temperature before you fill them.

SEAFOOD CREPES

Serves 4

For the filling
100 g/4 oz whitefish fillets
100 g/4 oz smoked cod fillet
225 g/8 oz mixed seafood, prepared, such as
  shelled clams, mussels, squid and peeled
  and deveined prawns
3 Tbsp butter
3 Tbsp flour
300 ml/½ pt milk
150 ml/¼ pt dry white wine
2 Tbsp fresh chives, chopped
1 Tbsp fresh tarragon, chopped
50 g/2 oz freshly grated Cheddar cheese

For the crêpes
100 g/4 oz plain flour
Pinch of salt
1 egg
300 ml/½ pt milk
Oil for frying

❶ Wash the fish and seafood mixture under cold running water and pat dry. Cut the fish into 2.5 cm/1 inch cubes. Put the fish and seafood in the top of a greaseproof paper-lined steamer, cover with a tight-fitting lid and steam over boiling water for 5 to 7 minutes until the fish is cooked right through.

❷ Meanwhile, melt the butter for the sauce and stir in the flour. Cook for 1 minute. Gradually stir in the milk and wine, and bring to the boil, stirring continuously until thickened.

❸ Remove the sauce from the heat and stir in the fish and seafood, herbs and cheese.

❹ Sieve the flour for the crêpes into a mixing bowl with the salt. Make a well in the centre and gradually whisk in the egg and milk to make a smooth batter. Heat a little oil in a 15 cm/6 inch crêpe pan, pour off into a dish and add a quarter of the batter, turning the pan to coat the base. Cook for 2 minutes and turn the crêpe. Cook for 1 minute and remove. Repeat with the remaining batter, heating oil in the pan for each crêpe.

❺ Roll the crêpes into cones and spoon the fish mixture into the centre. Arrange on a heatproof plate and put in the top of a prepared steamer. Cover and cook for 5 minutes. Serve immediately with lemon wedges and salad.

If lobsters are unavailable or beyond your budget, use cooked prawns in its place for an equally impressive salad. Serve with warm cheese or garlic bread.

HOT LOBSTER SALAD

Serves 4

Two 450 g/1 lb cooked lobsters
2 celery sticks, cut into julienne strips
1 medium red onion, halved and finely
   shredded
4 cobs baby corn, halved lengthwise
1 medium carrot, cut into julienne strips
50 g/2 oz mangetout, sliced
Mixed salad greens
Lime quarters, to garnish

For the dressing
2 Tbsp olive oil
1 Tbsp lime juice
1 Tbsp garlic wine vinegar
1 tsp prepared Dijon mustard
2 garlic cloves, peeled and crushed
1 Tbsp fresh dill, chopped

❶ Halve the lobsters and remove the meat. Cut into 2.5 cm/1 inch cubes. Lay a sheet of dampened greaseproof paper in the base of the steamer top and arrange the lobster and vegetables inside. Cover with a tight-fitting lid and steam over boiling water for 10 minutes until the vegetables are tender and the lobster is hot.

❷ Meanwhile, arrange the salad greens in a shallow serving bowl. Mix the dressing ingredients in a small saucepan and heat gently until hot.

❸ Spoon the lobster and vegetables onto the salad leaves and pour the dressing over the top. Garnish with dill and serve immediately.

Spicy crab makes a great filling for courgettes or other vegetables such as peppers and vegetable marrow. Use canned crab meat if fresh is unavailable.

SPICY CRAB-FILLED COURGETTES

Serves 4

4 large courgettes
1 small yellow pepper, seeded and finely
  chopped
2 celery sticks, finely chopped
1 Tbsp capers
1 Tbsp stoned black olives, chopped
450 g/1 lb crab meat
4 Tbsp mayonnaise
1 Tbsp lime juice
Zest of 1 medium lime
Few drops of Tabasco or other hot sauce
Salt and freshly ground black pepper
Pinch of cayenne pepper
50 g/2 oz freshly grated mozzarella cheese

❶ Trim the ends from the courgettes and blanch whole in boiling water for 7 to 8 minutes. Drain well and leave to cool.

❷ Cut courgettes in half lengthwise and scoop out the seeds with a teaspoon.

❸ Mix the remaining ingredients, except the mozzarella, together and spoon into the courgette shells. Sprinkle the cheese on top.

❹ Transfer the filled courgettes to a steamer tier, cover with a tight-fitting lid, and steam for 15 to 20 minutes or until hot and cooked through. Serve immediately with a crisp salad. For a crispy filling finish off under the grill.

Steaming is a great way to cook squid as it gives a tender texture. Don't skimp on the marinating time, because the ingredients will soak up the Mediterranean flavours for a fuller taste.

MEDITERRANEAN SQUID

Serves 4

8 large squid, cleaned
1 small red onion, cut into eight
16 black olives, stoned
2 large beef tomatoes,
seeded and chopped
100 g/4 oz feta cheese, cubed
2 Tbsp fresh coriander or oregano, chopped

For the marinade
2 Tbsp olive oil
2 Tbsp lemon juice
1 garlic clove, peeled and crushed
Freshly ground black pepper

For the sauce
300 ml/½ pt Greek-style yoghurt
50 g/2 oz cucumber, finely diced
2 garlic cloves, peeled and crushed
2 tsp lemon juice
Fresh oregano, chopped
Lemon zest, to garnish

❶ Wash the squid under running water and pat dry. Cut into rings. Put in a shallow glass dish with the onion, olives, tomatoes, feta cheese and herbs.

❷ Mix the marinade ingredients and pour over the squid mixture, turning to coat well. Cover and marinate for 1 hour, turning occasionally.

❸ Remove the ingredients from the marinade and arrange on a dampened sheet of greaseproof paper in the base of the steamer top. Bring the water to the boil in the base of the steamer and place the squid and remaining ingredients on top. Cover with a tight-fitting lid and cook for 5 minutes until the squid is tender.

❹ Meanwhile, mix the sauce ingredients together in a bowl and chill.

❺ Serve the squid with warm bread and the dressing on the side.

55

Fennel is a great accompaniment to succulent mussels, adding a subtle aniseed flavour that is perfect with seafood. Use white grape juice in place of wine as a non-alcoholic variation.

STEAMED MUSSELS WITH CREAMY FENNEL SAUCE

Serves 4

2 kg/4 lb mussels, scrubbed,
beards removed
1 small carrot, cut into julienne strips
1 small fennel bulb
2 garlic cloves, peeled and crushed
600 ml/1 pt fish stock

For the sauce
2 Tbsp butter
1 small red onion, finely diced
1 garlic clove, peeled and crushed
85 ml/3 fl oz dry white wine
1 Tbsp fresh mixed herbs, chopped
Freshly ground black pepper
85 ml/3 fl oz double cream

❶ Clean the mussels, removing the beards, and discarding any shells that open when tapped. Place the mussels in the base of the steamer with the carrot strips.

❷ Finely shred half of the fennel and add to the pan with the garlic and stock. Cover with a tight-fitting lid and steam for 5 minutes.

❸ Discard any unopened mussels and remove all the mussels and vegetables from the stock with a slotted spoon. Keep warm. Measure up 175 ml/6 fl oz of the stock and set aside.

❹ Meanwhile, melt the butter in a saucepan and sauté the onion and garlic for 2 minutes until softened. Add the wine, herbs, black pepper and cream. Pour in the 175 ml/6 fl oz of fish stock.

❺ Finely chop the remaining fennel and add to the pan. Bring to the boil and cook for 8 to 10 minutes.

❻ Spoon the mussels into warmed serving dishes and top with the vegetables. Serve with the wine and cream sauce.

Scallops are delicious with a mild creamy sauce, which enhances but does not overpower their flavour. Steaming scallops ensures that they have a perfect texture and are not overcooked.

SCALLOPS IN SAFFRON CREAM

Serves 4

20 fresh, prepared scallops
Juice and zest of 1 medium lemon
1 garlic clove, peeled and crushed
1 tsp fresh ginger, grated

For the sauce
150 ml/¼ pt double cream
4 Tbsp dry white wine
4 Tbsp fish stock
1 Tbsp fresh chives, chopped
Few saffron strands

❶ Rinse the scallops under running water and pat dry. Place in a shallow glass dish. Mix the lemon juice and zest, garlic and ginger, and pour over the scallops. Stir to coat, cover and marinate for 1 hour, turning occasionally.

❷ Remove the scallops from the marinade and transfer to a greaseproof paper-lined steamer tier. Cover and steam for 3 to 4 minutes until the scallops are cooked through.

❸ Meanwhile, heat the sauce ingredients in a small saucepan and cook for 5 to 7 minutes.

❹ Spoon the scallops onto warmed serving plates and serve with the sauce, fresh steamed vegetables and rice or noodles.

The silky sweetness of coconut milk combines with the fiery spices to make this prawn dish a perfect dinner party recipe. Reduce the quantity of chilli used for a milder dish or simply remove the seeds, where most of the "heat" is found.

SPICY GARLIC PRAWNS

Serves 4

300 g/10 oz uncooked prawns, peeled and
   deveined
2 large courgettes, cut into julienne strips
1 medium red chilli, finely chopped
1 medium carrot, cut into julienne strips
1 medium red pepper,
cut into julienne strips
2 medium tomatoes, seeded and chopped
2 Tbsp olive oil
1 tsp fresh ginger, grated
4 garlic cloves, peeled and crushed
Juice and zest of 1 medium lime
1 tsp ground turmeric
1 tsp ground coriander
1 tsp ground cumin
4 Tbsp coconut milk
1 Tbsp light soy sauce
225 g/8 oz dry egg noodles
2 Tbsp fresh coriander, chopped
Fresh coriander leaves, to garnish

❶ Rinse the prawns under running water and pat dry. Put in a shallow glass dish with the vegetables. Mix the oil, ginger, garlic, lime, spices, coconut milk and soy sauce together, and pour over the ingredients. Stir to coat, cover and marinate for 1 hour, turning occasionally.

❷ Half-fill the base of the steamer with water and bring to the boil. Cover the base of the steamer top with dampened greaseproof paper and add the prawns, vegetables and marinade. Place over the steamer base, cover with a tight-fitting lid and steam for 10 minutes. Put the noodles into the boiling water in the steamer base. Replace the prawns and cook for a further 5 minutes or until the noodles and prawns are cooked.

❸ Remove the steamer top and drain the noodles. Arrange on a warmed serving plate and top with the prawn mixture. Garnish with chopped coriander, and serve.

Steaming is an excellent way to preserve the moist goodness and flavour of poultry. All poultry is a good source of protein, vitamins and minerals and is one of the most popular meats in our diet. Most of the poultry is skinned before steaming, so further reducing the fat content and making it the perfect choice for those watching their waistlines.

Being so very versatile, it is easy to create a wide range of tempting dishes with chicken: it can be skewered for kebabs; marinated with flavour-enhancing ingredients such as citrus fruits, oil, fresh herbs and spices; stuffed, spiced or casseroled; or used as a simple risotto.

POULTRY

The caramelised pineapple gives this colourful dish a real look and taste of the Caribbean, and complements the spicy chicken perfectly.

CARIBBEAN CHICKEN

Serves 4

4 chicken breast fillets (100 g/4 oz each), skinned

Salt and freshly ground black pepper

Juice and zest of 1 medium lime

1 Tbsp olive oil

1 medium red onion, halved and thinly sliced

4 garlic cloves, peeled and crushed

2 tsp fresh ginger, grated

1 medium red chilli, chopped

2 large tomatoes, seeded and chopped

225 g/8 oz sweet potato, peeled and chopped

1 medium ripe plantain, chopped

600 ml/1 pt chicken stock

1 cinnamon stick

225 g/8 oz rice

2 Tbsp butter

2 Tbsp light brown sugar

1 small pineapple, cored and cut into 16 wedges

Fresh parsley, chopped, to garnish

1 Rinse the chicken under cold water and pat dry. Season with salt and pepper and roll in the lime juice and zest.

2 Heat the oil in the base of the steamer and sauté the chicken for 3 to 4 minutes, turning until sealed. Add the onion, garlic, ginger and chilli, and cook for a further 2 minutes.

3 Stir in the tomatoes, sweet potato and plantain. Add the stock and cinnamon, cover, and cook for 1 hour.

4 Meanwhile, boil the rice for 15 minutes and drain well. Line the steamer top with a clean damp tea towel and spoon in the rice. Cover with the lid and cook over the chicken mixture for 15 minutes until cooked through.

5 Melt the butter in a frying pan with the sugar and add the pineapple. Cook for 5 minutes, turning until hot and coated in syrup. Be careful not to burn.

6 Spoon the rice onto a warm serving plate and top with the chicken mixture. Serve with the hot pineapple and garnish with parsley.

This dish has quite a delicate flavour. Serve with steamed rice and vegetables for a refreshing summer meal. Mango chunks would be ideal in place of grapes.

GARLIC CHICKEN WITH CUCUMBER AND GRAPES

Serves 4

4 skinned chicken breasts
(about 100 g/4 oz each)
1 garlic clove
Salt and freshly ground black pepper
1 medium cucumber, cut into julienne strips
100 g/4 oz seedless red grapes, halved

For the sauce
150 ml/¼ pt chicken stock
6 Tbsp single cream
2 Tbsp fresh tarragon, chopped
1 egg yolk

● Rinse the chicken breasts under cold water and pat dry. Rub the garlic over both sides, season with salt and pepper and place in the bottom tier of the steamer with the garlic.

● Steam for 15 minutes.

● Place the cucumber and grapes in the second steamer tier over the chicken and cook both tiers for 5 minutes or until chicken is cooked.

● Meanwhile, mix all of the sauce ingredients, except the egg, in a small saucepan and heat gently, but do not boil. Remove from the heat and whisk in the egg.

● Remove the cucumber and grapes from the steamer and stir into the sauce. Transfer the chicken to warmed serving plates and serve with the sauce and fresh steamed vegetables.

This is a richly warming winter dish, and with its potato topping, a meal in itself. Drier than a traditional hot pot, it is also ideal made with lamb chops.

CHICKEN HOT POT

Serves 4

4 chicken pieces, boned, skinned and halved
(about 300 g/10 oz each)
2 medium carrots, thinly sliced
2 celery sticks, finely chopped
225 g/8 oz swede, roughly chopped
1 medium red onion, quartered and thinly
sliced
50 g/2 oz green beans, cut ino thirds
50 g/2 oz baby corn, halved lengthwise
2 Tbsp fresh thyme, chopped
1 bay leaf
150 ml/¼ pt chicken stock
6 Tbsp dry cider or apple juice
Salt and freshly ground black pepper
2 large potatoes, peeled and scrubbed

● Rinse the chicken pieces under running water and pat dry. Put with the vegetables, herbs, stock, and cider or apple juice in a heatproof dish which fits in the steamer top. Season well.

● Cover tightly with pleated foil and secure with string.

● Put the potatoes in salted boiling water in the base of the steamer, place the chicken mixture tier on top, cover tightly, and steam for 1 to 1½ hours or until cooked through.

● Remove the potatoes from the water after 10 minutes and slice thin. Arrange on dampened greaseproof paper in the upper steamer tier and steam over the chicken for 20 minutes, or until tender.

● Remove the potatoes and chicken from the steamer. Spoon the chicken and vegetables onto warmed serving plates and top with sliced potato. Serve with a fresh green salad and crusty bread.

Making a risotto in the base of a steamer means that the two tiers may be used to cook a first course and dessert at the same time. Be sure to use risotto rice, now widely available.

CHICKEN AND SAFFRON RISOTTO WITH LEEKS AND ASPARAGUS

Serves 4

4 Tbsp butter

2 medium leeks, finely chopped

2 garlic cloves, peeled and crushed

1 medium red pepper, diced

225 g/8 oz risotto rice

450 g/1 lb lean chicken, diced, skinned and boned

Few saffron strands

450 ml/³⁄₄ pt chicken stock

150 ml/¹⁄₄ pt dry white wine

8 baby corn, halved lengthwise

4 Tbsp frozen peas

Salt and freshly ground black pepper

4 Tbsp asparagus spears, cut into quarters

4 Tbsp freshly grated Parmesan cheese

❶ Melt the butter in the base of a steamer. Sauté the leek, garlic and bell pepper for 2 to 3 minutes, stirring. Add rice. Cook for 2 minutes.

❷ Rinse the chicken under running water and pat dry. Stir with the saffron into the pan. Mix the stock and wine together and pour in a third of the quantity. Bring to a boil, reduce to simmer, and cover with a tight-fitting lid for 20 minutes.

❸ Stir in the corn and peas, season, and add another third of the liquid. Cover again and cook for a further 20 minutes.

❹ Add the remaining liquid, the asparagus and cheese, cover and cook for 10 minutes, or until the rice is tender. Serve immediately.

Traditionally cooked in a large, shallow open frying pan and in large quantities, Paella is the flagship of Spanish cooking. By using your covered steamer base to cook the following variation, all of the aromatic flavours contained within the recipe are retained and the textures of the rice and vegetables are perfect. If saffron is unavailable, use a ¹/₂ teaspoon of turmeric in its place for colour.

PAELLA

Serves 4

450 g/1 lb boneless, skinned chicken, cubed
2 Tbsp olive oil
4 slices salami
1 large red onion, quartered and thinly sliced
2 garlic cloves, peeled and crushed
1 large red pepper, cubed
175 g/6 oz risotto rice
600 ml/1 pt chicken stock
Salt and freshly ground black pepper
Large pinch of cayenne pepper

Few saffron strands
100 g/4 oz peeled, deveined prawns
16 mussels, scrubbed, beards removed
50 g/2 oz peas
Fresh parsley, chopped, to garnish

❶ Rinse the chicken under running water and pat dry. Heat the oil in the base of the steamer and cook the chicken for 3 to 4 minutes, turning until browned. Add the salami, onion, garlic, red pepper and rice, and cook for a further 5 minutes, stirring.

❷ Add the stock and season with salt and pepper. Add the cayenne and saffron, cover, and steam over a gentle heat for 15 minutes.

❸ Add the remaining ingredients, replace the lid, and cook for a further 5 to 7 minutes until the chicken and rice are cooked through.

❹ Spoon into a warmed serving dish and garnish with chopped parsley.

Pecans and blue cheese are a great combination and make for a wonderful sauce with these colourful moist chicken pockets. Walnuts or macadamia nuts could be used in place of pecans.

STUFFED CHICKEN IN A BLUE CHEESE AND PECAN SAUCE

Serves 4

4 chicken escalopes (about 100 g/4 oz each)
Salt and freshly ground black pepper
4 Tbsp fresh wholemeal breadcrumbs
2 Tbsp pecans, chopped
5 spring onions, finely chopped
2 garlic cloves, peeled and crushed
1 small red pepper, finely chopped
2 tsp lemon juice
Zest of 1 medium lemon
2 Tbsp butter, melted

For the sauce
1 Tbsp butter
1 Tbsp plain flour
150 ml/¼ pt milk
6 Tbsp dry white wine
4 Tbsp soft blue cheese, crumbled
2 Tbsp pecans, chopped
4 Tbsp fresh watercress, chopped
4 Tbsp plain yoghurt
Lemon wedges and watercress, to garnish

❶ Rinse the chicken under running water and pat dry. Place between two sheets of greaseproof paper and beat with a mallet until 6 mm/ ¼ inch in thickness. Be careful not to pound too thin. Cut a slit in the side of each escalope to form a pocket. Season the inside of the pocket with salt and pepper.

❷ Mix the remaining stuffing ingredients together and spoon into the pockets, pressing in with the back of a spoon.

❸ Put the chicken pieces in the top of a steamer lined with damp greaseproof paper. Cover and steam for 15 minutes until the chicken is cooked through.

❹ Meanwhile, melt the butter for the sauce in a pan and add the flour. Cook for 1 minute and gradually stir in the milk and wine. Bring to the boil until the sauce thickens.

❺ Add the cheese, pecans, watercress and yoghurt, and heat gently until the cheese has melted.

❻ Remove the chicken from the steamer and place on a warmed serving plate. Spoon on the sauce and serve garnished with lemon and watercress.

Couscous is a cracked wheat which cooks light and fluffy. Steaming is the best method of cooking the grain, which is enhanced by the addition of butter to separate the grains after cooking.

CHICKEN COUSCOUS

Serves 4

1 kg/2¼ lb lean boneless chicken, cubed, skinned
1 Tbsp olive oil
1½ pts chicken stock
1 large red onion, cut into eight
2 garlic cloves, chopped
Pinch of saffron strands
½ cinnamon stick, bruised
4 medium tomatoes, seeded and quartered
2 large carrots, cut into chunks
½ large turnip, cut into eight
2 medium courgettes, thickly sliced
2 Tbsp raisins
1 tsp ground coriander
Large pinch cayenne pepper
Salt and freshly ground black pepper
350 g/12 oz couscous
2 Tbsp butter
Coriander sprigs, to garnish

❶ Rinse the chicken under running water and pat dry. Heat the oil in the steamer base and sauté the chicken, onion and garlic for 3 to 4 minutes until the chicken is sealed. Pour in chicken stock to just cover the meat and add the saffron, cinnamon, tomatoes, carrots, turnips, courgettes, raisins, coriander and cayenne. Season well, cover with a tight-fitting lid, and steam for 1¼ hours until the meat is tender and cooked through.

❷ Meanwhile, soak the couscous in a bowl of cold water for 20 minutes, 50 minutes before the meat is done. Drain well. Line the steamer top with a clean, damp tea towel and spoon in the couscous. Cover with the lid and place over the meat and vegetables in the base of the steamer. Steam for 30 minutes until the couscous is cooked through.

❸ Stir the butter into the couscous and separate with a fork to remove any lumps. Spoon onto a warmed serving plate and spoon the meat mixture on top. Garnish and serve.

Make these great chicken rolls in advance and store in the refrigerator for up to 4 hours, ready to cook, for a fast but impressive meal. Reheat by steaming for 7 to 10 minutes.

HERB AND MUSHROOM CHICKEN ROLLS

Serves 4

4 boneless chicken breasts, skinned
(about 100 g/4 oz each)
Salt and freshly ground black pepper
50 g/2 oz mushrooms, cleaned and chopped
2 spring onions, chopped
2 garlic cloves, peeled and crushed
1 small red pepper, finely chopped
6 Tbsp cream cheese
4 Tbsp cooked rice, preferably mix of wild
and long-grain rice

For the butter
6 Tbsp butter
2 garlic cloves, crushed
2 Tbsp fresh tarragon, chopped
1 Tbsp fresh parsley, chopped

❶ Rinse the chicken under running water and pat dry. Place between two sheets of greaseproof paper and beat with a mallet or rolling pin until 6 mm/¼ inch thick. Season.

❷ Mix together the mushrooms, spring onions, garlic, red pepper and cream cheese. Stir in the rice. Then spoon the filling along the length of the chicken and roll up. Secure with a cocktail stick and place in a steamer tier.

❸ Place the butter, garlic and herbs in a small heatproof bowl which fits the steamer tier, and set aside.

❹ Cover the chicken with a tight-fitting lid and steam for 20 minutes or until the chicken is cooked through.

❺ Five minutes before the chicken is cooked, place the butter mixture in its bowl, into a tier over the chicken, cover, and steam until melted and hot.

❻ Transfer the chicken to warmed serving plates and spoon the butter over the top. Serve immediately.

BASIL-WRAPPED MARINATED CHICKEN KEBABS

Serves 4

350 g/12 oz boneless chicken, skinned

4 Tbsp walnut oil

1 Tbsp balsamic vinegar

Juice of ½ medium orange

2 Tbsp clear honey

1 large bunch fresh basil

1 shallot, chopped

1 medium yellow pepper, cubed

12 button mushrooms, cleaned

12 cherry tomatoes

1 medium head chicory or
heart of 1 small lettuce

Oak leaf lettuce

For the dressing

2 Tbsp walnut oil

2 Tbsp garlic wine vinegar

1 tsp prepared mustard

2 Tbsp clear honey

Juice of ½ medium orange

Salt and freshly ground black pepper

❶ Rinse the chicken under running water and pat dry. Cut into 2.5 cm/1 inch cubes and put in a shallow glass dish. Mix the walnut oil, vinegar, orange juice, honey, a few basil leaves and the shallot, and pour over the chicken, turning to coat. Cover, and leave to marinate for 1 hour, turning occasionally.

❷ Remove the chicken from the marinade and wrap each piece in a basil leaf. Thread onto four halved wooden skewers with the yellow pepper, mushrooms and cherry tomatoes. Arrange on a heatproof plate in the base of the steamer top, cover with a tight-fitting lid and steam for 15 minutes until the chicken is cooked through.

❸ Meanwhile, mix the dressing ingredients in a small saucepan and gently heat. Arrange the salad leaves on a serving plate and place the cooked kebabs on top.

❹ Drizzle the warm dressing over and garnish with freshly ground pepper.

Steaming a whole chicken is the perfect way to obtain a really succulent result, and helps the meat to take on the wonderful Thai flavourings. If lime leaves are unavailable, use large mint or basil leaves.

WHOLE THAI-SPICED CHICKEN WITH A COCONUT SAUCE

Serves 4

1.4 kg/3 lb oven-ready chicken

1 large lemon, halved

2 tsp fresh ginger, grated

1 large red chilli, finely chopped

2 garlic cloves, peeled and crushed

2 tsp lemon grass, finely chopped

Juice of 1 medium lime

1 Tbsp fresh coriander, chopped

Salt and freshly ground black pepper

½ tsp Thai spice powder (chilli powder, dried garlic, ginger, ground coriander, ground cinnamon, ground cumin, star anise and garlic powder)

2 Tbsp vegetable oil

150 ml/¼ pt dry white wine

Lime leaves

For the sauce

150 ml/¼ pt chicken stock

150 ml/¼ pt coconut milk

❶ Wash the chicken inside and out, and pat dry. Place the halved lemon inside the cavity and transfer to a deep glass dish.

❷ Mix the remaining marinade ingredients together (except the lime leaves) and pour over the chicken. Cover tightly and leave to marinate for at least 2 hours, turning occasionally.

❸ Prepare the steamer, lining the base of the upper tier with the lime leaves. Remove the chicken from the dish, reserving the marinade, and place on top of the lime leaves. Cover and steam for 1 to 1¼ hours until cooked through.

❹ Meanwhile, heat the marinade in a small saucepan with the stock and coconut milk. Serve with the chicken and jasmine rice.

Your butcher, or the gourmet meat section at a well-stocked supermarket, should have poussins, which are small, very young chickens. If unavailable, use small chicken pieces or quarters.

POUSSIN WITH CHILLI NECTARINES

Serves 4

4 poussins (about 350 g/12 oz each)

For the marinade
2 garlic cloves, peeled and crushed
1 red chilli, chopped
1 shallot, finely chopped
4 Tbsp olive oil
1 Tbsp balsamic vinegar

For the sauce
2 Tbsp butter
2 large ripe nectarines, chopped into
    medium chunks
1 medium red chilli, finely chopped
2 spring onions, chopped
3 Tbsp dry sherry
250 ml/8 fl oz chicken stock

Ripe nectarines, orange and chilli, for garnish
Fresh watercress, to garnish

❶ Rinse the poussins under running water and pat dry. Cut down each side of the backbone, and remove the bone (or ask your butcher to do this). Lay the birds breast side down on a chopping board and press down to flatten them out.

❷ Lay the birds in a shallow glass dish, mix the marinade ingredients together and pour over the birds, turning to coat. Cover and leave to marinate for 1 hour, turning occasionally.

❸ Remove the poussins and lay them in the base of the steamer top on a sheet of dampened greaseproof paper. Cover and steam for 25 minutes or until cooked through.

❹ Meanwhile, for the sauce, melt the butter in a small pan and add the remaining sauce ingredients. Bring to the boil, reduce the heat to simmer and cook for 10 minutes.

❺ Remove the poussins from the steamer and place on a warm serving dish. Spoon the sauce over, garnish and serve with boiled potatoes.

There are many ready-to-eat dried fruits available which add to this dish's intense flavour. Choose a wide mixture such as pears, mango, apple, sultanas or cherries for best results.

CHICKEN WITH SPICY DRIED FRUIT

Serves 4

12 chicken wings (about 75 g/3 oz each)
175 g/6 oz mixed dried fruits, such as
  apricots, prunes, sultanas, peaches,
  roughly chopped
2 Tbsp dry sherry
6 Tbsp orange juice
1 tsp ground coriander
½ tsp ground cumin
½ tsp ground cinnamon
½ tsp chilli powder
2 garlic cloves, peeled and crushed
2 Tbsp clear honey
2 Tbsp butter

For the rice
6 Tbsp long-grain rice
600 ml/1 pt chicken stock
2 spring onions, chopped
Pinch of turmeric
1 small red chilli, chopped
Orange segments, to garnish

❶ Rinse the chicken under running water and pat dry. Place in a shallow glass dish with the fruit, sherry, orange juice, spices, garlic and honey. Cover and leave to marinate for 1 hour, turning occasionally.

❷ Meanwhile, cook the rice in the stock with the spring onions, turmeric and chilli in the base of the steamer for 15 minutes. Drain well and spoon into four ramekins or moulds.

❸ Remove the chicken from the dish, reserving the marinade, and place in the bottom tier of the steamer. Put the rice moulds in the next tier and place on top. Cover with a tight-fitting lid and steam for 20 minutes or until the chicken is cooked through.

❹ Meanwhile, heat the marinade in a small saucepan and whisk in the butter to give a glossy sauce.

❺ Transfer the chicken to warm plates; spoon the sauce over. Turn a rice mould onto each plate and garnish with orange segments. Serve immediately.

The poussins are spiced with paprika and cinnamon, and served with a rich, gamy sauce. Cornish hens, quails and even chicken portions can also be used.

POUSSIN WITH SPICY RAISIN SAUCE

Serves 4

2 poussins of equal size, halved (about
   350–450 g/12–15 oz each)
Juice of 1 large lime
1 tsp cinnamon
1 tsp paprika

For the sauce
150 ml/¼ pt red wine
6 Tbsp chicken stock
3 Tbsp raisins
½ tsp cinnamon
2 Tbsp butter

❶ Rinse the poussins under water and pat dry. Rub with the lime juice, cinnamon and paprika, and place in a steamer tier over boiling water. Cover and cook for 25 minutes or until cooked through.
❷ Meanwhile, place all of the sauce ingredients, except the butter, in a small saucepan and bring to the boil. Boil rapidly to reduce by half.
❸ Whisk the butter into the sauce a little at a time, until sauce is smooth and glossy.
❹ Remove the poussins from the steamer and serve glazed with the sauce.

This dish has a slightly Oriental flavour which perfectly complements the tender poussins. Serve with steamed scented rice and/or mixed vegetables.

POUSSIN WITH ORANGE AND GINGER

Serves 4

4 poussins (about 350 g/12 oz each)
Juice and zest of 2 medium oranges
2.5 cm/1 inch piece ginger, finely shredded
2 garlic cloves, peeled and crushed
2 Tbsp fino sherry
1 Tbsp light soy sauce
Several spring onions, shredded
4 Tbsp butter
1 orange, peeled and segmented, to garnish

❶ Rinse the poussins under running water and pat dry. Put in a deep dish. Mix the orange juice and half of the zest, the ginger, garlic, sherry and soy sauce together, and pour over the poussins, turning to coat. Cover and marinate for 1 hour, turning occasionally.
❷ Remove the birds from the dish, reserving the marinade.
❸ Arrange the spring onions in the base of the steamer top on a dampened piece of greaseproof paper, add the poussins and cover tightly.
❹ Steam for 30 minutes or until cooked through. Meanwhile, heat the marinade in a small pan and whisk in the butter to make a rich glossy sauce.
❺ Remove the poussins from the steamer and arrange on warmed serving plates. Pour the sauce over, garnish, and serve with rice and/or fresh lightly stir-fried vegetables.

Turkey is a great meat all-year-round, full of taste and low in fat. In this recipe it takes on a slightly Oriental flavour.

TURKEY KEBABS WITH ONION RELISH

Serves 4

350 g/12 oz lean, skinned turkey, cubed
1 Tbsp dark soy sauce
1 Tbsp light soy sauce
2 Tbsp fino sherry
1 medium red chilli, finely chopped
2 garlic cloves, peeled and crushed
1 medium courgette, cut into
    2.5 cm/1 inch chunks
8 artichoke hearts, canned
8 small cherry tomatoes
1 medium lime, cut into quarters

For the relish
2 Tbsp butter
1 Tbsp oil
1 large onion, halved and sliced
6 Tbsp vegetable stock
1 Tbsp dry sherry
1 tsp cornflour
1 Tbsp fresh parsley, chopped
Freshly ground black pepper

❶ Rinse the turkey under running water and pat dry. Place in a shallow glass dish with the soy sauces, sherry, chilli and garlic. Cover and marinate for 1 hour, turning occasionally.

❷ Thread the turkey and vegetables onto four halved wooden skewers and place in the top of the steamer. Steam for 15 to 20 minutes.

❸ Melt the butter with the oil in a saucepan and fry the onion for 10 minutes until browned. Add all of the remaining ingredients except the cornflour, cover, and cook for 10 minutes.

❹ Blend the cornflour with 4 teaspoons cold water and whisk into the relish. Bring to the boil, stirring until thickened and clear. Serve immediately with the kebabs and a green salad.

This is quite a rich dish filled with strong flavours both in the meat and the sauce. Chicken, turkey, or any game birds could be used in place of the duck. Serve with boiled potatoes as a foil against the duck's richness.

MADEIRA DUCK WITH MIXED WILD MUSHROOMS

Serves 4

4 boneless duck breasts (about 175 g/
   6 oz each), skinned

3 garlic cloves, peeled and crushed

300 ml/½ pt chicken stock

8 Tbsp Madeira

4 Tbsp cherry jam

250 g/½ lb mixed mushrooms, cleaned and
   thinly sliced

2 Tbsp fresh parsley, chopped

Salt and freshly ground black pepper

1 Tbsp cornflour

1 Rinse the duck under running water and pat dry. Slice the duck breasts and place in a shallow glass dish. Mix one third of the garlic cloves, the stock, Madeira and jam together, and spoon over the duck. Cover and marinate for 1 hour, turning occasionally.

2 Line the steamer top with dampened greaseproof paper and add the mushrooms. Sprinkle with the remaining garlic and the parsley.

3 Remove the duck breasts from the dish, reserving the marinade, and place on top of the mushrooms. Cover and steam for 40 minutes or until cooked through.

4 Meanwhile, heat the marinade in a small saucepan. Blend the cornflour with 2 tablespoons of cold water to make a paste and whisk into the marinade. Bring to the boil, stirring until thickened and clear. Arrange a few mushrooms on each of four serving plates, top with the duck breasts, pour the sauce over and serve with steamed rice.

Duck is a rich, strong-flavoured meat ideal countered by a citrus flavour such as lime. Ginger adds warmth. Any fruit jelly, such as currant, apple or gooseberry may be used in place of the port-and-cranberry jelly. The dish would also be ideal with turkey and chicken.

GINGER-LIME DUCK ON A BED OF SPINACH

Serves 4

4 boneless duck breasts, skinned (about
    175 g/6 oz each)
4 Tbsp port-and-cranberry jelly
100 g/4 oz fresh baby spinach, washed
1 large carrot, cut into julienne strips
2 celery sticks, cut into julienne strips
50 g/2 oz mangetout
1 medium red onion, quartered and thinly
    sliced
2 medium limes
2.5 cm/½ inch piece fresh ginger, grated
450 ml/¾ pt chicken stock
150 ml/¼ pt red wine
Lime zest and wedges, and parsley, to garnish

❶ Rinse the duck breasts under running water and pat dry. Brush with the jelly, coating both sides, and set aside.

❷ Lay the spinach in the base of a greaseproof paper-lined steamer tier and top with the remaining vegetables, the juice and zest of 1 lime, the ginger, and duck breasts.

❸ Pour the stock and wine into the base of the steamer with the remaining lime juice, and bring to the boil. Place the duck over the stock, cover with a tight-fitting lid, and steam for 25 to 30 minutes until the duck is cooked through.

❹ Remove the duck and vegetables from the steamer and keep warm. Boil the sauce to reduce by half. Serve the duck on the bed of vegetables with the sauce poured over. Garnish and serve. Excellent with rice or small boiled potatoes.

*S*teaming is the perfect cooking method for tender lean cuts of meat, of any size that will fit in the steamer. As a general rule, any meat that you would grill is suitable for steaming.

Remember too that the pieces of meat should be roughly of equal size. Always check that meats are thoroughly cooked before serving, and that the juices run clear. Adjust cooking times accordingly. With steaming, a moist, gentle cooking method, meats retain their natural juices and flavours, although some recipes use marinades or sauces to enhance these. There are simple recipes, well-marinated dishes, en papillote, kebabs, and a variety of dishes reminiscent of a number of international cuisines.

MEAT

A rich marinade gives the pork a tangy, slightly Oriental flavour and makes a lovely glaze for the cooked meat and potatoes. The pork should be sliced across the grain for extra tenderness.

PORK TENDERLOIN WITH POTATO CROUTE

Serves 4

350 g/12 oz pork fillet, sliced

2 Tbsp dark soy sauce

2 Tbsp clear honey

1 Tbsp sherry

2 Tbsp orange juice

1 garlic clove, peeled and crushed

2 large potatoes, peeled

1 medium carrot, cut into julienne strips

4 spring onions, chopped

Orange wedges, to serve

1 Cut the pork into thin slices and place in a shallow glass dish. Mix together the soy sauce, honey, sherry, orange juice and garlic, and pour over the pork, turning to coat. Cover and leave to marinate for 2 hours.

2 Meanwhile, cook the potatoes in boiling salted water in the steamer base for 5 minutes. Remove with a slotted spoon and slice very thinly. On a heatproof plate, arrange the potatoes in four circles, overlapping the slices, and place in the upper steamer tier.

3 Remove the pork from the marinade and place in the base of the lower steamer tier on dampened greaseproof paper. Top with the carrots and spring onions.

4 Place the pork over the steamer base, followed by the potatoes. Cover with a tight-fitting lid and steam for 25 minutes until the pork and potatoes are cooked through.

5 Meanwhile, in a separate pan, heat the marinade until reduced to a glossy sauce.

6 Transfer the potato croûtes to four warm serving plates and top each with pork and vegetables. Spoon the glaze over the top, garnish with orange wedges, and serve with freshly steamed green vegetables.

This recipe uses classic goulash ingredients, but is a drier version – ideal served with mashed or sautéed potatoes. Tender beef or lamb are ideal substitutes for pork, and plain yoghurt may be used instead of soured cream.

HUNGARIAN PORK

Serves 4

300 g/10 oz pork tenderloin, trimmed and thinly sliced

2 Tbsp butter

1 medium onion, cut into eight

2 garlic cloves, peeled and crushed

2 medium carrots, cut into julienne strips

4 large tomatoes, seeded and chopped

4 Tbsp pork or vegetable stock

2 tsp paprika

150 ml/5 fl oz soured cream

2 Tbsp fresh parsley, chopped

❶ Place all of the ingredients, except the soured cream and parsley, in a deep, heatproof bowl which fits into the steamer top. Put in the steamer and cover with a tight-fitting lid.

❷ Steam for 30 minutes until the meat is tender and cooked through.

❸ Add the soured cream and parsley to the bowl, stirring well. Replace the lid, and steam for a further 5 minutes. Serve with mashed or sautéed potatoes, or noodles.

*Perfect for a quick family supper, this recipe is delicious
made with either cider or apple juice, but be sure to use
unsweetened as this will affect the final flavour. Remember
to slice pork across the grain for a tender result.*

PORK FILLET WITH CIDER

Serves 4

450 g/1 lb pork tenderloin, trimmed and
   thinly sliced
2 medium leeks, halved lengthwise and sliced
8 baby corn, halved lengthwise
8 baby carrots, halved lengthwise
150 ml/¼ pt unsweetened apple cider
   or juice
2 Tbsp fresh sage, chopped
7 Tbsp double cream
Salt and freshly ground black pepper

1 Cut pork into thin slices. Place in centre of a large square of foil.

2 Bring the sides of the foil up and fold to make a parcel, leaving the
top open.

3 Add the leeks, corn and carrots, and pour in the cider. Add the sage
and seal the top of the parcel.

4 Transfer the parcel to a steamer tier, cover with a tight-fitting lid and
steam for 15 minutes.

5 Add the cream to the parcel and season to taste. Cover with the lid
and steam for a further 5 minutes or until the pork is cooked through.
Serve with rice or mashed potatoes.

*This dish makes full use of the steamer, cooking the pork
and vegetables over the noodles for an easy and nutritious,
low-fat supper.*

ORIENTAL PORK AND VEGETABLES

Serves 4

450 g/1lb pork tenderloin, trimmed
   and sliced
1 medium carrot, cut into julienne strips
50 g/2 oz mangetout
1 medium red pepper, thinly sliced
2 celery sticks, cut into julienne strips
1 medium leek, halved and thinly sliced
2 garlic cloves, peeled and crushed
Juice and zest of 1 medium orange
3 Tbsp dry sherry, such as fino
2 Tbsp light soy sauce
2.5 cm/½ inch piece fresh ginger, grated
1½ pts vegetable stock
300 g/10 oz dry egg noodles

1 Place the pork and vegetables in a shallow glass dish. Mix the
remaining ingredients (except the stock and noodles) together and
pour over the ingredients in the dish. Cover and leave to marinate for
at least 1 hour, turning occasionally.

2 Transfer the ingredients, including the marinade, to a heatproof dish
which fits the top of the steamer.

3 Put the stock in the base of the steamer. Cover with a tight-fitting
lid and steam over the stock for 20 minutes.

4 Add the noodles to the stock, replace the upper tier, and continue
steaming for a further 5 minutes until the pork and noodles are
cooked. Take care not to overcook the noodles.

5 Drain the noodles and place in a warm serving bowl. Top with the
pork and vegetables, and serve immediately.

Dim sum are so easy to make and are great as an impressive party food or as a snack or starter. The thin dough is very simple to make, ensuring minimum effort for maximum impact.

PORK DIM SUM

Serves 4

For the dough
225 g/8 oz plain flour
1 egg
2 tsp cold water
For the filling
175 g/6 oz minced pork
75 g/3 oz button mushrooms, cleaned and finely chopped
3 spring onions, chopped
½ small carrot, finely chopped
1 celery stick, finely chopped
2 Tbsp light soy sauce
1 tsp light sesame oil
1 tsp Chinese five-spice powder

For the dip
2 Tbsp dark soy sauce
1 medium green chilli, chopped
½ tsp dark sesame oil
2 tsp brown sugar
1 Tbsp sherry

❶ Sift the flour into a mixing bowl and stir in the egg and water to make a firm dough. On a floured surface, roll into a sausage shape and cut into 28 slices.

❷ Roll each slice into a 7.5 cm/3 inch round.

❸ Mix the filling ingredients together in a bowl and spoon into the centre of each dough circle. Dampen the edge of each circle with water and fold up the sides to encase the filling, pinching the top together.

❹ Put the dim sum in a stacking steamer lined with a clean damp teatowel, cover with the lid, and steam for 25 minutes until cooked through.

❺ Meanwhile, mix the dip ingredients together and place in a serving bowl. Serve the dim sum, garnished with spring onions and chilli.

If you don't like blue cheese, add any soft but strongly flavoured cheese in its place for an equally delicious result. Cottage cheese may be sieved and used instead of ricotta cheese for a healthier alternative.

BLUE CHEESE EGG POTS WITH GARLIC SAUSAGE

Serves 4

6 Tbsp soft blue cheese
4 Tbsp milk
2 Tbsp fresh parsley, chopped
Salt and freshly ground black pepper
250 g/8 oz ricotta cheese
1 medium tomato, seeded and chopped
100 g/4 oz garlic sausage, chopped
4 eggs

❶ Crumble the blue cheese into a mixing bowl and stir in the milk, parsley, and salt and pepper.

❷ Gradually blend in the ricotta cheese and stir in the tomato and sausage. Spoon the mixture into four ramekins and break an egg into each dish.

❸ Place the dishes in the steamer tiers, cover with a tight-fitting lid and steam for 6 to 8 minutes or until the egg is cooked, as desired. Serve immediately with toasted bread, or salad.

A filling and delicious lunch or supper dish, this variation on a fried rösti is also healthier, as there is no additional fat used. Vary the cheeses used according to personal taste, but be sure to use strongly flavoured varieties.

CHEESE AND HAM RÖSTI

Serves 4

900 g/1½ lb potatoes, peeled
100 g/4 oz smoked ham, cut into thin strips
100 g/4 oz freshly grated Cheddar cheese
50 g/2 oz blue cheese, crumbled
3 Tbsp shelled walnuts, chopped
120 ml/4 fl oz double cream or yoghurt
3 eggs, beaten
2 Tbsp fresh parsley, chopped
Salt and freshly ground black pepper

❶ Grate the potatoes into a sieve and press well to remove excess water. Transfer to a mixing bowl. Add all of the remaining ingredients and mix well. Press into the base of a shallow, heatproof dish which fits into the steamer top.

❷ Cover with foil and place in the steamer, place a tight-fitting lid on top, and cook for 45 minutes or until the potatoes are cooked through. Serve immediately with a crisp salad.

This is such a simple dish, perfect for children or for a quick supper or light lunch. Other cooked meats, such as salami, may be used in place of the ham.

SMOKED HAM AND EGGS EN COCOTTE

Serves 4

100 g/4 oz fresh spinach
Butter, for greasing
100 g/4 oz cooked smoked ham, cubed
4 eggs
Pinch of cayenne pepper
4 Tbsp single cream

1 Blanch the spinach in a small amount of boiling water until just cooked, and drain well, squeezing out any excess moisture.

2 Lightly grease four ramekins and place the spinach in the base of each.

3 Top with the ham and then break an egg into each dish. Sprinkle with cayenne pepper and spoon the cream on top.

4 Transfer the ramekins to the steamer tiers, cover with a tight-fitting lid and steam for 6 to 8 minutes or until the eggs are cooked, as desired. Serve with hot toast.

Steaming ribs gives a wonderfully tender result and a terrific flavour, accentuated here by a spicy sauce. Rubbing the ribs with salt before you start removes any excess moisture and juices which would otherwise come out during steaming and dilute the sauce. Be sure to rinse the ribs well and pat dry to remove the salt.

SPICY SPARERIBS

Serves 4

1½ kg/3 lb pork spareribs

1 Tbsp salt

150 ml/5 fl oz chicken or pork stock

2 Tbsp dark soy sauce

1 tsp ground ginger

2 tsp dark sesame oil

2 Tbsp garlic, peeled and finely chopped

2 medium red chillies, very finely chopped

2 tsp dark brown sugar

4 Tbsp clear honey

1 Tbsp tomato purée

2 Tbsp dry sherry

350 g/12 oz long-grain white rice

2 Tbsp fresh coriander, chopped

1 Rinse ribs under cold water and pat dry. Rub the ribs with the salt and leave for 30 minutes. Rinse thoroughly and pat dry. Fill the steamer base with water and bring to the boil. Add the ribs and cook for 10 minutes. Drain, discarding the water in the steamer.

2 Transfer the ribs to a heatproof bowl which fits the steamer top. Mix the stock, soy sauce, ginger, sesame oil, garlic, chillies, sugar, honey, tomato purée and sherry, and pour over the ribs.

3 Place the ribs over the prepared steamer base, cover with a tight-fitting lid and cook for 1 hour or until cooked through.

4 Meanwhile, halfway through the rib cooking time, add the rice to the steamer base water and cook for 15 minutes. Reduce the heat slightly and cook for a further 15 minutes until tender and fluffy. Remove the rice from the water before this if you prefer rice with a "bite". Stir in the coriander and spoon onto a warmed serving plate. Top with the ribs and keep warm. Place the marinade juices in a small saucepan and bring to the boil. Boil rapidly to reduce by half and pour over the ribs. Serve immediately.

A Cajun Creole pilaf which was created in the eighteenth century, Jambalaya is thought to have derived its name from the Spanish word for ham – jamon, an essential ingredient of early recipes. Today, smoked sausage is used for flavour and chilli provides the spice element. An economical dish, it's lower in fat than most recipes, and steaming makes it quicker to cook, with the added advantage of a sealed pan retaining all of the exquisite flavours within the dish.

JAMBALAYA

Serves 4

50 g/2 oz butter

1 large yellow pepper, medium chopped

1 large red pepper, medium chopped

1 large red onion, quartered and thinly sliced

2 celery sticks, thinly sliced

3 garlic cloves, peeled and crushed

1 large red chilli, finely chopped

3 large tomatoes, seeded and finely chopped

1 Tbsp tomato purée

Few drops of Tabasco Sauce

100 g/4 oz mixed long-grain white and
    wild rice

Salt and freshly ground black pepper

1½ pts vegetable stock

450 g/1 lb large peeled, cooked prawns

350 g/12 oz smoked sausage, medium diced

75 g/3 oz peas

❶ Melt the butter in the base of the steamer pan and sauté the peppers, onion, celery, garlic and chilli for 3 minutes, stirring.

❷ Add the tomatoes, tomato purée, Tabasco Sauce and rice, and season to taste. Stir in the stock and cover with a tight-fitting lid.

❸ Cook gently for 15 to 20 minutes. Add the prawns, sausage and peas, replace the lid, and continue cooking for a further 5 to 7 minutes until the rice is cooked through. Serve.

Steaming this classic recipe produces a flavourful and moist dish. Use minced beef as an alternative to the traditional lamb. Serve with a fresh, crisp salad and warm crusty bread.

MOUSSAKA

Serves 4

1 large aubergine
Salt
3 Tbsp olive oil
1 medium onion, halved and thinly sliced
2 garlic cloves, peeled and crushed
450 g/1 lb cooked lamb, finely chopped
497 g/15 oz can chopped tomatoes
2 tsp dried mixed herbs
1 Tbsp Worcestershire sauce
2 Tbsp butter
2 Tbsp plain flour
300 ml/10 fl oz milk
1 egg, separated
50 g/2 oz freshly grated Cheddar cheese
2 Tbsp freshly grated
Parmesan cheese

❶ Slice aubergine thin and place in a colander. Sprinkle with salt and leave for 30 minutes. Rinse under cold water and pat dry.

❷ Heat the oil in a frying pan and cook the aubergine for 2 to 3 minutes. Remove from the pan and set aside. Add the onion and garlic to the frying pan and cook over medium heat for 2 to 3 minutes, until softened.

❸ Remove the onion and garlic from the heat. Stir the lamb, tomatoes and herbs and Worcestershire sauce into the frying pan and mix well.

❹ Arrange a layer of aubergine slices in the base of a deep heatproof serving dish. Top with meat mixture and the remaining aubergine.

❺ Melt butter in a saucepan. Whisk in flour. Stirring constantly, cook for 1 minute. Gradually add milk. Bring to the boil, stirring.

❻ Remove the pan from the heat and stir in the egg yolk and cheese. Whisk the egg white in a clean bowl until peaking and gently fold into the sauce. Pour over the meat mixture and cover with pleated foil, secured with string to prevent steam escaping and to secure a tight fit.

❼ Place the dish in the top of the steamer, cover tightly with the lid, and steam for 20 minutes. Serve sprinkled with the cheese, and a salad.

The cucumber and yoghurt sauce lends a Greek tone to this tender lamb – a very refreshing fusion of flavours. The vegetables make for a very colourful dish.

LAMB WITH CHILLED YOGHURT SAUCE

Serves 4

900 g/2 lb lean lamb, cubed

3 garlic cloves, peeled and crushed

3 Tbsp olive oil

Juice and zest of 1 medium lemon

1 Tbsp fresh oregano, chopped

6 Tbsp red wine

Salt and freshly ground black pepper

1 medium yellow pepper, cubed

2 Tbsp stoneless black olives, quartered

1 medium courgette, cut into julienne strips

1 medium red onion, cut into eight

2 large tomatoes, seeded and chopped

6 Tbsp lamb stock

For the sauce

6 Tbsp cucumber, diced

2 garlic cloves, peeled and crushed

1 Tbsp fresh chives, chopped

300 ml/½ pt Greek-style yoghurt

❶ Put the lamb in a shallow glass dish. Mix together the garlic, 1½ tablespoons of oil, lemon juice and zest, oregano, wine and salt and pepper. Pour over the lamb, cover and marinate for 2 hours, turning occasionally.

❷ Remove the lamb from the marinade with a slotted spoon, reserving the marinade. Heat the remaining oil in a frying pan and brown the lamb, turning for 2 to 3 minutes. Add the yellow pepper, olives, courgette, onion and tomatoes, and cook for 2 to 3 minutes. Spoon the contents of the pan into a heatproof dish.

❸ Pour the stock into a saucepan along with the reserved marinade. Bring to the boil and cook until reduced to a thickened sauce (about 4 to 5 minutes). Pour over the lamb. Cover the dish tightly with pleated foil secured with string and place in the steamer top. Cover with a tight-fitting lid and steam for 30 to 35 minutes until the meat is cooked through.

❹ Meanwhile, mix the sauce ingredients together and chill until required. Serve with the lamb and freshly steamed rice.

If you don't have Madeira, use a dry sherry such as fino: the result will be equally delicious, although it is worth treating yourself to the real thing.

LAMB WITH MADEIRA SAUCE

Serves 4

4 lamb tenderloins (about 100 g/4 oz each)
    4 Tbsp (50 ml) dry Madeira, such as Sercial
2 Tbsp lamb stock
1 tsp Worcestershire sauce
1 Tbsp fresh thyme, chopped
1 Tbsp tomato purée
75 g/3 oz mushrooms,
washed and thinly sliced
1 medium orange pepper, thinly sliced
8 pearl onions
50 g/2 oz green beans, halved
2 Tbsp butter

1 Place the lamb in a shallow glass dish with the Madeira, stock, Worcestershire sauce, thyme and tomato purée. Cover and leave to marinate for at least 1 hour.

2 Remove the lamb from the dish, reserving the marinade, and place in a greaseproof paper-lined steamer tier with the vegetables. Cover with a tight-fitting lid and steam for 20 minutes or until cooked through.

3 Meanwhile, heat the marinade in a small saucepan and whisk in the butter to make a glossy sauce. Serve with the lamb and vegetables and a bowl of freshly steamed rice.

This spicy peppercorn-encrusted lamb is ideal with a milder vegetable dish and mashed potatoes. For a milder dish, halve the quantity of peppercorns used.

LAMB WITH BACON PEPPERCORN SAUCE ON A BED OF CABBAGE

Serves 4

50 g/2 oz mixed peppercorns
3 tsp prepared Dijon mustard
650 g/1½ lb boneless shoulder of lamb,
    cubed
100 g/4 oz green cabbage, shredded
150 ml/¼ pt lamb or chicken stock
150 ml/¼ pt red wine
4 slices smoked bacon, diced (about
    100 g/4 oz)
1 tsp light brown sugar
2 Tbsp butter
Salt and freshly ground black pepper

1 Crush the peppercorns with a mortar and pestle or in a plastic bag using a rolling pin. Spread 2 teaspoons of the mustard over the lamb and coat in all but 1 tablespoon of the peppercorns.

2 Arrange the cabbage in the centre of a large square of foil and place the lamb on top. Bring up the sides to make a parcel, sealing the top.

3 Place the parcel in the steamer tier, cover with a tight-fitting lid, and steam for 20 minutes or until cooked through. Leave the parcel sealed.

4 Mix the stock, remaining mustard and peppercorns, wine, bacon and brown sugar in a small saucepan. Cook gently for 5 to 7 minutes.

5 Gradually whisk the butter into the wine mixture to make a glossy sauce. Serve the lamb on the bed of cabbage with the sauce drizzled over.

Lamb chops are ideal for steaming as they are small and take little time to cook. Reduce the cooking time if you prefer lamb rare. If possible, marinate the lamb for a longer period of time, up to 4 hours, for a stronger, richer, flavour.

LAMB CHOPS WITH SPICY PEACH RELISH

Serves 4

8 lamb chops (about 75 g/3 oz each in
   weight)

2 Tbsp olive oil

2 garlic cloves, peeled and crushed

1 Tbsp lemon juice

1 Tbsp balsamic vinegar

2 Tbsp clear honey

2 sprigs fresh rosemary

For the sauce

2 Tbsp butter

3 peaches, skinned, stoned and chopped

4 spring onions, chopped

150 ml/¼ pt lamb or vegetable stock

150 ml/¼ pt peach juice

1 Tbsp raisins

½ tsp ground cinnamon

1 tsp ground ginger

1 Tbsp cornflour

❶ Put the lamb chops in a shallow glass dish. Mix the oil, garlic, lemon juice, vinegar, honey and rosemary, and pour over the lamb. Cover and marinate for at least 1 hour, turning occasionally.

❷ Meanwhile (for the sauce) melt the butter in a pan and add the remaining ingredients except the cornflour. Transfer to a shallow heatproof dish which fits the steamer.

❸ Remove the lamb from the marinade and add to the sauce in the dish. Cover with plastic wrap and steam for 20 minutes or until the lamb is cooked through. Remove the lamb from the steamer and keep warm. Pour the sauce into a small saucepan. Blend the cornflour to a paste with 2 tablespoons cold water and stir into the sauce. Bring to the boil, stirring until thickened and clear. Spoon over the lamb and serve with new potatoes and green vegetables.

The lamb takes on the rich, warm qualities of the port and rosemary for a full-flavoured dish. Madeira or sherry could work equally as well as port, and any complementary preserve could be used.

LAMB FILLET WITH PORT AND GARLIC SAUCE

Serves 4

450 g/1 lb boneless shoulder of lamb, cubed
2 sprigs fresh rosemary
1 garlic clove, peeled and crushed
2 Tbsp olive oil

For the sauce
150 ml/¼ pt port
50ml/2 fl oz lamb stock
2 garlic cloves, peeled and thinly sliced
1 tsp sugar
2 Tbsp redcurrant jelly
2 tsp cornflour
Rosemary sprigs, to garnish

❶ Place the lamb in a shallow glass dish. Mix the rosemary, garlic and oil together, pour over the lamb and mix well. Cover and leave to marinate for 1 hour, turning occasionally.

❷ Meanwhile, pour the port and stock into a small saucepan and add the garlic, sugar and redcurrant jelly. Heat slowly until the jelly dissolves.

❸ Blend the cornflour with 4 teaspoons of cold water and stir into the sauce. Bring to the boil until thickened and clear.

❹ Remove the lamb and rosemary from the marinade and spoon into a heatproof dish which fits the top of the steamer. Pour the sauce over the lamb and cover with a tight-fitting lid.

❺ Steam the lamb for 15 to 20 minutes until cooked through. Serve with fresh steamed vegetables and garnish with rosemary sprigs.

Beef and horseradish are a classic combination of flavours, and this dish is no exception. The sauce may be made in advance and reheated for serving. Creamed horseradish may be made by mixing 4 tablespoons prepared horseradish sauce and 1 tablespoon soured cream together, or bought ready-made in a pot.

MEATBALLS WITH HORSERADISH SAUCE

Serves 4

450 g/1 lb minced beef

1 egg

1 celery stick, finely chopped

1 Tbsp tomato purée

1 Tbsp fresh basil, chopped

1 Tbsp stoned green olives,
finely chopped

1 spring onion, finely chopped

1 tsp Worcestershire sauce

Salt and freshly ground black pepper

4 Tbsp fine breadcrumbs

For the sauce

2 Tbsp butter

2 Tbsp plain flour

300 ml/½ pt milk

150 ml/¼ pt dry white wine

1 large bunch basil, leaves only,
   washed and shredded

2 Tbsp prepared creamed horseradish sauce

To serve

100 g/4 oz brown rice

600 ml/1 pt vegetable stock

1 Put the ingredients for the meatballs in a food processor or blender and blend for 30 seconds until combined, or mix well by hand. Roll into walnut-sized balls.

2 Put the rice and stock in the base of the steamer and bring to the boil. Arrange the meatballs on a sheet of dampened greaseproof paper in the top of the steamer and cover with a tight-fitting lid. Cook with the rice for 20 minutes until the rice and meatballs are cooked through. Check the rice after 15 minutes to make sure it doesn't overcook.

3 Meanwhile, melt the butter for the sauce in a pan and whisk in the flour. Cook, stirring, for 1 minute. Gradually stir in the milk and wine, and bring to the boil, stirring constantly.

4 Add the remaining sauce ingredients and cook for 5 minutes. Blend in a food processor for 30 seconds until smooth.

5 Drain the rice and spoon onto a warmed serving plate. Arrange the meatballs on top and spoon on the sauce. Serve immediately.

If a less than prime cut of beef is used, tenderise the meat with a mallet before cooking. The basil gives an aromatic flavour to the dish, but if unavailable, oregano may be used.

PEPPERED BEEF FILLET WITH BASIL TOMATO SAUCE

Serves 4

450 g/1 lb fillet steak
2 Tbsp peppercorns
For the sauce
4 Tbsp dry sherry
200 ml/7 fl oz passata
2 spring onions, sliced
2 Tbsp fresh basil, shredded
1 tsp light brown sugar

1 Tenderise the meat with a mallet and cut into four equal-sized pieces.

2 Crush the peppercorns in a mortar and pestle or in a plastic bag with a rolling pin and press into the beef on both sides.

3 Transfer the beef to a steamer tier, cover with a tight-fitting lid, and steam for 15 minutes or until cooked through.

4 Meanwhile, place all of the sauce ingredients in a small saucepan and bring to the boil. Reduce the heat and simmer for 10 minutes.

5 Remove the beef from the steamer and serve with the sauce and fresh steamed vegetables, and boiled potatoes.

Although this recipe is a little time-consuming, it is well worth the effort. Feel free to use other meats and vegetables that you have to hand for variation of fillings. It is important to cover the dough with a damp cloth to allow it to rest without drying out.

SPICY BEEF RAVIOLI

Serves 4

For the ravioli dough

225 g/8 oz plain flour

50 g/2 oz semolina

Pinch of salt

4 tsp olive oil

2 eggs, beaten

3–4 Tbsp milk

For the filling

100 g/4 oz minced beef

1 small onion, finely chopped

1 small carrot, finely diced

½ tsp ground cumin

½ tsp ground coriander

Pinch of paprika

2 tsp fresh thyme, chopped

1 Tbsp tomato purée

Salt and freshly ground black pepper

For the sauce

6 Tbsp butter

3 tsp lemon juice

3 Tbsp vegetable stock

2 Tbsp red wine

Pinch of dry mustard

1 garlic clove, peeled and crushed

3 Tbsp fresh mixed herbs, chopped

Parmesan strips, to garnish

❶ Make the pasta dough by sifting the flour into a mixing bowl. Add the semolina and salt and make a well in the centre.

❷ Place the oil, beaten eggs, and 1 tablespoon of milk in the well and gradually mix into the flour and semolina to make a firm dough, adding more milk if necessary to give a smooth dough. On a lightly floured board, knead the dough and cover with a damp cloth for 30 minutes.

❸ Mix the filling ingredients together and put on a heatproof plate. Place in the top of a warm steamer, cover with a tight-fitting lid and steam for 20 minutes until cooked through. Allow to cool.

④ Cut the pasta dough into 8 equal pieces. Dust a worksurface with flour and roll one piece of the pasta dough to a 20 x 10 cm/8 x 4 inch rectangle; the dough should be quite thin, but still hold together. Repeat with the other seven pieces of dough. Brush four pieces of dough with water and spoon small quantities of the filling at regular intervals on the dough.

⑤ Place the other four sheets of dough on top, pressing down between the piles of filling to make sealed squares. Cut out each square with a knife or fluted cutter. Leave to dry on a clean tea towel for 2 hours.

⑥ Fill the steamer base with water and bring to the boil. Cook the ravioli in the water for 5 minutes. Remove with a slotted spoon and transfer to a heatproof bowl, small enough to fit into the steamer.

⑦ Mix the sauce ingredients together and add to the bowl. Place in the steamer top and cover with a tight-fitting lid. Steam for 5 to 7 minutes until cooked through. Serve immediately.

Fresh calf's liver is ideal for steaming. It will remain moist and tender and, served in a mustard wine sauce, is a real treat. Try it, especially if you think you've never liked liver. Full of iron, it's a highly nutritious meat.

LIVER IN A HERBED MUSTARD SAUCE

Serves 4

450 g/1 lb calf's liver
150 ml/¼ pt red wine
1 garlic clove, peeled and crushed
2 tsp fresh sage, chopped
1 medium leek, finely sliced
1 large carrot, cut into julienne strips

For the sauce
1 Tbsp butter
1 Tbsp plain flour
5 Tbsp plain yoghurt or single cream
2 Tbsp fresh sage, chopped
Salt and freshly ground black pepper

① Cut the liver into thin strips and place in a shallow glass dish. Mix the wine, garlic and sage, and pour over the liver. Cover and marinate for 1 hour, turning occasionally.

② Remove the liver, reserving the marinade, and place in a greaseproof paper-lined steamer tier with the vegetables. Cover with a tight-fitting lid and steam for 10 minutes or until cooked through.

③ Meanwhile, melt the butter for the sauce in a small pan and stir in the flour. Remove from the heat and add the marinade, yoghurt or cream and sage. Return to the heat and heat gently without boiling, stirring until thickened. Season to taste.

④ Place the liver and vegetables on a warmed plate, and top with the sauce. Garnish with sage and serve with boiled potatoes.

*I*f you're looking for a plain steamed pudding, you've come to the wrong book! The following desserts are a mile away from the traditional, stodgy steamed desserts of yesteryear.

Many of the delicious fruits now available are perfect for steaming, be it on a skewer, in a brulée, marinated or served with a luxurious sauce. These desserts are light and refreshing, packed with colour, flavour and natural goodness—although there are a couple of "naughty but nice" recipes for those of us who really can't resist.

DESSERTS

Adding sweet potato to bananas gives great colour, texture and flavour to this warm dessert, perfect for a cold winter evening.

STEAMED BANANAS IN ORANGE SAUCE

Serves 4

175 g/6 oz sweet potato,
peeled and cubed

4 large ripe bananas cut into pieces

2 Tbsp light brown sugar

8 Tbsp orange juice

Zest of 1 medium orange

2 Tbsp orange liqueur

Fresh mint or lemon balm leaves, to decorate

Double cream or vanilla yoghurt, to serve

❶ Boil the sweet potato in water in the base of the steamer for 10 minutes. Remove with a slotted spoon.

❷ Cut four large sheets of foil and place ¼ of the sweet potato in the centre of each.

❸ Cut the bananas in half lengthwise and place one banana on top of each parcel. Sprinkle with sugar and fold up the sides of the foil but don't seal.

❹ Spoon the orange juice and zest, and the liqueur into the parcels and fold the top of the foil over to seal.

❺ Steam the fruit in the top of the steamer, covered, for 5 minutes until hot and the sugar has melted. Decorate with fresh mint, and serve with double cream or yoghurt.

This is a seasonal dish, capturing the wonderful warm flavours and aromas of winter. It may be made with segmented sweet oranges when clementines are unavailable.

FRESH FIGS WITH CLEMENTINES

Serves 4

8 small clementines, peeled, with pith
    removed

6 Tbsp orange juice

2 Tbsp brandy

1 Tbsp grenadine syrup (optional)

1 Tbsp light brown sugar

16 medium fresh figs

Plain yoghurt, to serve

Fresh mint sprigs and pared orange or lemon
    zest, to decorate

❶ Place the clementines in a heatproof dish and place in a steamer tier.

❷ Pour the orange juice, brandy and grenadine, if using, into a small saucepan, add the sugar and heat gently to dissolve. Bring to the boil.

❸ Add the figs to the clementines, pour the syrup over and cover with a tight-fitting lid. Steam for 15 minutes.

❹ Spoon the fruit into a serving dish, with a little of the syrup around. Decorate and serve.

This combination of fruit makes a real splash of colour and flavour on the plate. If you prefer crêpes – and are skilled at making them – they work equally well.

FRUIT PUREE WITH WAFFLES AND CREAM

Serves 4

2 kiwi fruit
1 papaya
1 small pineapple

To serve
150 ml/¼ pt plain yoghurt
1 medium passion fruit
4 prepared waffles
Fresh mint sprigs, to decorate

● Halve the kiwi fruit and scoop the flesh onto the centre of a foil square. Bring up the sides of the foil to make a sealed parcel.

● Peel, halve, seed and chop the papaya, place the flesh in another foil square and seal well.

● Peel, core and chop the pineapple, place the flesh into another foil parcel, and place all three parcels in the top of the steamer. Cover with the lid, and steam for 10 minutes until hot.

● Either press each fruit separately through a strainer or blend in a food processor, until smooth. Cut the passion fruit in half and scoop out the seeds and flesh. Mix with the yoghurt and serve with the three fruit syrups, spooned over the waffles. Decorate with mint, and serve.

Brulée is an all-time favourite dessert with most people, and very simple to prepare and cook in a steamer. Tinned plums will work, though of course fresh is always preferred. Fruits such as cherries, peaches or nectarines may also be used as alternatives.

PLUM BRULEE

Serves 4

4 medium ripe plums, pitted and chopped
2 Tbsp (25 mL) Kirsch
2 cups (450 mL) heavy cream
1 tsp (5 mL) vanilla extract
4 egg yolks
2 Tbsp (25 mL) almonds, chopped
3 Tbsp (45 mL) demerara or brown sugar

● Place the plums in the base of four lightly buttered ramekins and spoon a quarter of the Kirsch over each.

● Heat the cream in a saucepan until just below boiling point but do not boil. Remove from the heat and stir in the vanilla extract, egg yolks and nuts.

● Pour the cream over the plums and place in the top of the steamer. Cover and steam for 10 minutes. Remove from the steamer and chill for 4 hours.

● Sprinkle the tops of the brulées with sugar and cook under a hot grill for 3 to 4 minutes until the sugar caramelises, but do not let it blacken and burn. Return the brulée to the refrigerator until the topping hardens, and serve, decorated with fresh plums.

This is a little like a berry pie with a nutty batter top. Choose a good variety of fresh, seasonal berries for flavour. A dollop of vanilla extract in the cream or yoghurt is a nice touch.

BERRY CLAFOUTI

Serves 4

650 g/1½ lb mixed berries, such as blackberries, raspberries and strawberries, washed

2 Tbsp light brown sugar

4 Tbsp toasted flaked almonds

For the batter

175 g/6 oz self-raising flour

2 Tbsp ground almonds

1 tsp baking powder

2 Tbsp light brown sugar

150 ml/¼ pt milk

1 egg, separated

Yoghurt or cream, to serve

❶ Put the fruit in the base of a heatproof, shallow dish which fits the top of the steamer, and sprinkle the sugar on top.

❷ Mix all of the batter ingredients together except the egg white. Whisk the egg white until peaking and gently fold into the batter. Spoon over the fruit in the bowl and scatter the almonds on top.

❸ Cover the dish with pleated foil and secure with string. Cook, covered, in the steamer for 1 to 1¼ hours or until the batter is cooked through.

❹ Remove the foil and serve immediately with yoghurt or cream.

Once filled, this cake should be stored in the refrigerator and eaten within a day, which won't be a problem. If using fresh banana slices to decorate the cake top, be sure first to mix them up with a bit of lemon juice, to prevent discolouration.

PECAN-BANANA CAKE

Serves 4

100 g/4 oz butter
100 g/4 oz light brown sugar
2 eggs, beaten
3 medium bananas, mashed
4 Tbsp self-raising wholemeal flour
4 Tbsp self-raising flour
100 g/4 oz pecans, chopped
4 Tbsp sultanas
1 Tbsp lemon juice
4 Tbsp plain yoghurt

❶ Lightly grease the bases of two 17.5cm/7 inch sponge cake tins. Line with greaseproof paper.

❷ Cream the butter and sugar until light, and gradually beat in the eggs. Stir in the mashed bananas and fold in the flours, nuts, sultanas, lemon juice and yoghurt. Spoon into the prepared tins and cover with pleated greaseproof paper, secured with string.

❸ Place a cake tin in each tier of the steamer, cover and steam for 1¼ hours, changing the tiers over halfway through cooking time, or until cooked through.

❹ Allow the cakes to cool slightly before turning out to cool completely on a wire rack.

❺ Mix the banana, icing sugar, yoghurt, lemon juice and cream cheese together for the filling, and spread over the top of the each cake. Sandwich together and decorate the top with chopped pecan nuts and dried bananas, slice and serve.

Chocolate sponge pudding must be top of the list with most people, especially when served hot with whipped cream flavoured with rum.

HOT CHOCOLATE PUDDING

Serves 4

100 g/4 oz plain chocolate, grated
2 Tbsp milk
2 Tbsp brandy
225 g/8 oz self-raising flour
100 g/4 oz butter or margarine, softened
4 Tbsp dark brown sugar
2 Tbsp ground almonds
2 eggs, beaten
1 Tbsp coffee extract or very strong coffee, cooled
Icing sugar and grated
chocolate, for decoration

❶ Lightly butter a 1-litre/2-pint pudding basin. Slowly melt the chocolate with the milk and brandy in a bowl over hot water.

❷ Sieve the flour into a mixing bowl and cut in the butter until the mixture resembles breadcrumbs. Stir in the sugar, ground almonds, eggs, coffee extract and melted chocolate mixture.

❸ Spoon the batter into the pudding basin, cover with pleated greaseproof paper and foil secured with string. Steam, covered, for 1½ to 2 hours or until a knife inserted in the centre comes out clean.

❹ Turn the pudding out onto a warmed serving plate, dust with icing sugar and sprinkle with grated chocolate. Serve hot with custard or cream.

Dried fruits have such an intense flavour, and take on other flavours such as orange and alcohol with wonderful results. Serving them as kebabs makes them even more tempting.

SPICED FRUIT KEBABS

Serves 4

12 stoned prunes

12 dried apricots

8 pieces dried mango

8 dried apple rings

Juice of 1 medium orange

2 Tbsp orange liqueur or sweetened orange juice

1 tsp ground cinnamon

Pinch ground nutmeg

4 cloves

For the sauce

75 g/3 oz cream cheese

8 Tbsp plain yoghurt

1 Tbsp clear honey

❶ Place all of the fruit in a shallow glass dish. Mix the juice of the orange, the liqueur or sweetened orange juice, and spices, and pour over the fruits. Cover and leave to marinate for 1 hour, turning occasionally.

❷ Remove the fruit from the marinade, reserving the liquid, and thread onto four halved wooden skewers. Place in the steamer over boiling water, cover with a tight-fitting lid, and steam for 10 minutes.

❸ Meanwhile, mix the marinade with the cream cheese, yoghurt and honey.

❹ Remove the skewers from the steamer and serve with the sauce.

This dish is great served hot or cold with thin wafers, almond thins or tuiles. A rich red wine could be used in place of the port. Arrowroot, a thickening agent that doesn't yield a chalky taste is preferable to cornflour.

PEARS IN PORT

Serves 4

4 large ripe sweet pears

150 ml/¼ pt ruby port

6 Tbsp light brown sugar

2 Tbsp cherry jam

½ tsp ground cinnamon

Grated zest of 1 medium orange

2 tsp arrowroot or cornflour

Orange segments, to decorate

❶ Peel the pears and remove the cores. Place in a deep dish which fits the steamer.

❷ Heat the port, sugar, jam, cinnamon and orange zest in a pan until the jam melts. Pour over the pears.

❸ Cover with pleated greaseproof paper, secure with string and cover with the lid. Steam for 15 to 18 minutes until the pears are cooked through but not falling apart. Remove from the syrup and place on serving plates.

❹ Transfer the port to a small saucepan and whisk in the arrowroot. Bring to the boil, stirring constantly until the sauce is thickened and clear. Spoon the sauce over the pears and decorate with orange segments. Serve warm.

This is a really attractive way to serve an old favourite. Adding mint to the rice gives it a subtle flavour which is particularly enjoyable with the fresh raspberry sauce.

RICE PUDDING CASTLES WITH RASPBERRY COULIS

Serves 4

150g/5 oz pudding rice
250 ml/8 fl oz milk
50 ml/2 fl oz double cream
4 Tbsp demerara sugar
Pinch of grated or ground nutmeg
2 Tbsp fresh mint, chopped
1 tsp vanilla extract
2 Tbsp chopped toasted hazelnuts

For the sauce
225 g/8 oz raspberries, fresh, or thawed
   if frozen
2 Tbsp icing sugar
1 tsp almond essence

❶ Mix the rice, milk, cream, sugar, nutmeg, mint, vanilla and nuts, and spoon into four moulds. Cover with pleated foil secured with string.

❷ Place the moulds in the steamer tiers, cover with the lid, and steam for 1 hour or until set.

❸ Meanwhile, put the sauce ingredients in a food processor or blender, and purée until smooth. Press through a sieve to remove any seeds. Turn the puddings out onto serving plates and spoon the sauce over. Serve immediately.

Usually a lengthy dish to prepare, this Charlotte Russe is quick, simple and really delicious. Be sure to pack the sponge fingers tightly around the basin to keep the coffee custard in place. You can find ready-made sponge fingers at most supermarkets. Serve with 100 ml/4 fl oz whipped double cream or thick yoghurt flavoured with 2 teaspoons brandy.

COFFEE CHARLOTTE RUSSE

Serves 4

2 large ripe pears, peeled,
cored and chopped
4 Tbsp brandy
175 g/6 oz sponge fingers
450 ml/³/₄ pt full-cream milk
4 eggs
200 g/7 oz soft light brown sugar
2 Tbsp coffee liqueur
Brandy-flavoured cream or yoghurt, to serve

❶ Soak the pears in the brandy, turning frequently, for at least 20 minutes.

❷ Line the sides of a greased 1-litre/2-pint straight-sided mould or casserole dish with sponge fingers and fill the base with the remaining fingers, chopped.

❸ Add the pears and brandy to the centre of the mould.

❹ Heat the milk until almost boiling, but do not let boil. Remove from the heat.

❺ Beat the eggs and sugar together, and stir in the coffee liqueur. Stir into the milk, and gently pour into the mould. Cover with clingfilm and place in the steamer.

❻ Cover with a tight-fitting lid and steam over simmering water for 40 to 50 minutes until set. Leave to cool completely before unmoulding to serve. Serve with brandy-flavoured cream or yoghurt.

This is a great alternative way to serve fruit salad; served warm, the flavours meld together wonderfully. Use any variety of fruit you have to hand if preferred, making sure there is a good combination of colours and that the fruit is fairly firm in texture.

STEAMED TROPICAL FRUIT KEBABS

Serves 4

1 large star fruit, thickly sliced
1 medium papaya
1 small cantaloupe melon
12 seedless green grapes
2 large slices fresh pineapple

For the marinade
2 Tbsp Kirsch
150 ml/¼ pt orange juice
Juice of 1 medium lemon
2 Tbsp caster sugar
2 tsp arrowroot or cornflour

To serve
Small prepared sweet pancakes or crêpes
Double cream or plain yoghurt

❶ Place the sliced star fruit and grapes in a shallow glass dish. Seed and chop the papaya, and add to the dish. With a melon baller, scoop the flesh from the melon and add to the dish. Cut the pineapple into chunks and add to the fruit.

❷ Mix all of the marinade ingredients and pour over the fruit. Cover with clingfilm and chill for 2 hours, stirring occasionally.

❸ Remove the fruit from the marinade, reserving the liquid. Thread the fruit onto four halved wooden skewers, and set in the steamer top. Place the pancakes in the lower tier of the steamer, cover and cook for 10 minutes until hot.

❹ Meanwhile heat the marinade in a small pan. Whisk in the arrowroot and bring to the boil, stirring until thickened and clear. Arrange the pancakes on small serving plates, and top with cream. Serve the kebabs with the pancakes and syrup.

The slight tartness of the apricot sauce served with these stuffed, steamed apples complements well the apples' cinnamony sweetness. Other fruit, such as peaches or mango, would make an equally delicious sauce. Choose an apple suitable for baking.

STUFFED APPLES WITH APRICOT SAUCE

Serves 4

4 medium cooking apples (about 225 g/
  8 oz each)
2 tsp light brown sugar
1 Tbsp dried apricots, chopped
1 Tbsp sultanas
1 Tbsp dried dates, stoned and chopped
¼ tsp ground cinnamon
¼ tsp grated fresh or ground nutmeg
2 Tbsp butter, melted

For the sauce
6 fresh or tinned apricots, peeled,
  stoned and chopped
Juice of 1 medium orange
½ tsp almond extract
1 Tbsp light brown sugar
Fresh mint sprigs, to decorate

❶ Core the apples. Mix the dried fruits, sugar and spices in a bowl, and stir in the butter to bind.

❷ Spoon the mixture into the cored apples and place in a steamer tier.

❸ Mix all of the sauce ingredients together in a heatproof bowl which fits the steamer and place in the second tier, over the apples.

❹ Place both tiers over boiling water, cover with a tight-fitting lid, and steam for 15 minutes until the apples are cooked through and the skins begin to split around the centre.

❺ Keep the apples warm and pour the sauce into a food processor or blender. Blend for 30 seconds until smooth. Transfer the apples to a serving plate and spoon the sauce around. Decorate and serve immediately.

This is such a simple yet truly wonderful dessert. Served with almond biscuits, the apples are irresistible and sure to impress. While you could, at a pinch, use an inexpensive apple brandy, Calvados is well worth the cost (and great with fresh, sliced apples).

CALVADOS APPLES WITH MINT CREAM

Serves 4

4 Tbsp Calvados or apple brandy
Juice of 2 large oranges
1 Tbsp orange liqueur
2 Tbsp clear honey
4 medium red eating apples (about 150 g/ 5 oz each)
½ cinnamon stick, bruised

For the cream
150 ml/¼ pt double cream, whipped
150 ml/¼ pt plain yoghurt
1 Tbsp clear honey
2 Tbsp fresh mint, chopped

❶ Bring the Calvados, orange juice, liqueur and honey to the boil in a small saucepan.

❷ Meanwhile, cut the apples into quarters and remove the cores. Place in a heatproof bowl and pour the syrup over the top. Add the cinnamon stick and cover with pleated foil.

❸ Place the bowl in the steamer, cover with a tight-fitting lid, and steam for 15 minutes until the apples are tender, but not soft.

❹ Meanwhile, whip the cream and fold in the remaining ingredients together. Transfer to a serving dish and chill until required.

❺ Remove the apples from the Calvados syrup and arrange on serving plates. Spoon the sauce over the top, decorate with mint and serve with the cream on the side.

These individual puddings have a comforting warmth of flavours, beautifully set off by the tangy sauce. Add 2 tablespoons of strong coffee for an alternative dessert and 2 tablespoons of extra flour.

GINGER-ORANGE PUDDINGS

Serves 4

115 g/4½ oz butter or margarine, softened

100 g/4 oz light brown sugar

2 eggs, beaten

2 pieces crystallised ginger, finely chopped

2 Tbsp golden syrup

½ tsp baking soda

2 Tbsp orange juice

Zest of 1 medium orange

Pinch of ground ginger

225 g/8 oz plain flour

To serve

300 ml/½ pt plain yoghurt

Zest and juice of ½ small orange

2 tsp icing sugar, sieved

Orange zest and segments, to decorate

❶ Grease the insides of four ramekins using 1 tablespoon of the butter. Beat the remaining butter and the sugar together until light and fluffy. Gradually beat in the eggs, ginger, syrup, baking soda, orange juice and zest, and ground ginger to taste.

❷ Fold in the flour and spoon into the prepared ramekins. Cover with pleated foil and secure with string.

❸ Place the dishes in the steamer, cover with a tight-fitting lid and cook for 30 minutes or until a toothpick inserted into the puddings comes out clean.

❹ Meanwhile, mix the sauce ingredients together and chill. Turn the cooked puddings out onto a serving plate, decorate with orange zest and segments and serve with the sauce.

Crème caramel is a classic favourite. Usually cooked in the oven, it is perfect when steamed, and takes on a new twist with rich, sugar-glazed pineapple. Any firm fruit could be glazed and served in this way, such as mango, pears or peaches.

CREME CARAMEL WITH GLAZED PINEAPPLE

Serves 4

200 g/7 oz sugar
4 Tbsp cold water
400 ml/14 fl oz full-cream milk
3 eggs

For the pineapple
2 Tbsp butter
1 Tbsp dark brown sugar
4 rings fresh pineapple, cubed
   (about 300 g/10 oz each)

❶ Place 4 tablespoons of the sugar in a heavy saucepan with the water, and heat until the sugar dissolves. Increase the heat until the sugar syrup turns dark brown, being careful not to burn. Remove from the heat and pour into four ramekins, turning to coat the base and sides.

❷ Heat the milk until almost boiling. Do not boil or the custard will not set properly and will cook. Beat the remaining sugar and eggs together, and gradually pour in the milk.

❸ Pour the custard into the ramekins and then wrap each dish in clingfilm.

❹ Place in the steamer tier and cover with a tight-fitting lid. Cook over simmering water for 10 minutes, or until set. Leave to cool completely before unmoulding to serve.

❺ Before serving, melt the butter in a frying pan and add the sugar. Once the sugar has dissolved, stir in the pineapple pieces and cook for 4 to 5 minutes until glazed. Serve with the unmoulded crème caramels.

Pears and chocolate are a classic combination. Be sure to choose ripe pears and four of roughly equal size. Orange liqueur or strong cooled coffee could be used as a flavouring instead of the dark rum.

PEARS WITH RUM AND CHOCOLATE SAUCE

Serves 4

4 medium sweet, ripe pears

Juice of ½ medium orange (reserve zest to decorate)

150 g/5 oz dark chocolate

2 Tbsp dark rum

120 ml/4 fl oz double cream

Grated dark and white chocolate, to decorate

❶ Peel the pears and brush them with the orange juice. Put the pears in the first steamer tier.

❷ Break the chocolate into a heatproof bowl which fits inside the steamer tier. Add the rum and cream, cover with pleated foil and place over the pears. Cover with a tight-fitting lid.

❸ Cook the pears and sauce ingredients for 15 to 20 minutes or until the pears are cooked through, but not falling apart.

❹ Stir the chocolate sauce to combine the ingredients. Spoon the pears onto serving plates and top with the sauce. Decorate and serve.

This is one of those really quick desserts which is filled with both flavour and colour, and can be prepared and cooked almost on the spur of the moment with fruit you have in the house such as apples, pears or bananas. Use the syrup from the stem ginger to flavour the fruit.

HOT MANGO AND KIWI IN GINGER SYRUP

Serves 4

2 large ripe mangoes, peeled, stoned and cubed

3 ripe kiwi fruit, peeled and cut into eight

2 pieces crystallised stem ginger, each cut into eight

6 Tbsp ginger syrup

Juice of 1 medium lime

Lime zest, to decorate

Ginger snaps and yoghurt, to serve

❶ Place the fruit in the centre of a large square of foil. Bring up the sides, folding to form an open parcel.

❷ Mix the remaining ingredients together and pour over the fruit. Seal the parcel and place in the steamer.

❸ Cover with a tight-fitting lid and steam for 10 minutes. Remove from the steamer, decorate with lime zest and serve with ginger snaps and plain or yoghurt.

These individual puddings benefit from marinating in the alcohol and fruit juice. The fruit may be prepared up to 4 hours in advance and left to stand, for an easy dessert. Use a variety of fruit such as cherries, pears, apples, mangoes and pineapple for a really interesting dish.

MIXED FRUIT COBBLER WITH BRANDY SAUCE

Serves 4

For the fruit
300 g/10 oz mixed dried fruit, chopped
3 Tbsp brandy
4 Tbsp orange juice
1 tsp allspice
For the batter
2 eggs
2 Tbsp plain flour
3 Tbsp sugar
300 ml/½ pt milk

For the sauce
6 Tbsp granulated sugar
3 Tbsp boiling water
3 Tbsp brandy
2 Tbsp unsalted butter

1 Soak the fruit in the brandy, orange juice and allspice for 1 hour. Spoon into the base of four individual dishes.

2 Beat the eggs and whisk in the flour and then the sugar. Whisk in the milk to make a smooth batter.

3 Pour the batter over the fruit and wrap each dish in clingfilm.

4 Place the dishes in the steamer, cover with a tight-fitting lid and cook for 20 minutes or until the batter has set.

5 Meanwhile make the sauce. Dissolve the granulated sugar in a heavy pan and increase the heat until the sugar turns brown. Be careful not to burn. Remove from the heat and add the boiling water and the brandy. Return to the heat.

6 Gradually whisk in the butter, stirring constantly, until fully incorporated and glossy. Serve with the puddings.

This chapter is designed to show how versatile and economical the steamer is. If you have an electric steamer with several stacking tiers and rice bowl, you will be able to create complete meals just using the one steamer, all timed to perfection.

Using recipes chosen from the previous chapters, the following are suggested menus for you to try, but feel free to experiment and substitute your own favourites, and you'll soon discover how simple and delicious "Steam Cuisine" really is.

MENUS

MENU 1

• Pork Dim Sum • Quick Salmon with Pesto • Steamed Bananas in Orange Sauce

1½ hrs	1 hr	35–40 mins	30 mins	10 mins
Make up the pesto sauce, cover and store in the refrigerator. Prepare the Dim Sum ready to cook and place in the steamer tier. Make up the dip.	Boil sweet potato for Steamed Bananas in Orange Sauce. Prepare the remaining ingredients except the bananas.	Finish Steamed Bananas in Orange Sauce, seal the parcels ready for cooking.	Cook the Dim Sum in the prepared steamer for 25 mins.	Fill steamer base, cook pasta with salmon over the top for 10 mins. Drain pasta and keep warm with salmon. Serve Dim Sum. Serve salmon and pasta. Cook bananas for 5 mins and serve.

MENU 2

• Hot Lobster Salad • Caribbean Chicken • Plum Brulée

4½ hrs	1½ hrs	1 hr	20 mins	5 mins
Heat water in steamer base. Prepare brulée, steam for 10 mins. Remove and chill in the refrigerator for 4 hours.	Prepare chicken, sauté in base of steamer, add remaining ingredients, cover and cook for 1 hour. Boil the rice for chicken for 15 mins. Drain and set aside.	Prepare lobster and vegetables, place in steamer ready to cook. Mix dressing ingredients in a pan. Top brulée with sugar, grill 3–4 mins. Return to refrigerator.	Cook rice in steamer over chicken for 15 mins. Set lobster salad over rice, cook 15 mins. Place salad greens in bowl. Cook the pineapple for 5 mins.	Serve lobster salad starter. Keep chicken, rice and pineapple warm, serve as main course. Serve brulée as dessert.

MENU 3

• Courgette and Beans with Garlic and Mint • Paella • Crème Caramel with Glazed Pineapple

2 hrs	1 hr	30–40 mins	5 mins
Prepare and cook the Crème Caramel. Chill in the refrigerator ready to serve. Prepare the pineapple for the dessert.	Prepare Paella ingredients, sauté the chicken, salami, garlic, pepper and rice 5 mins. Add stock, seasoning, cayenne and saffron.	Cover Paella, cook over gentle heat for 15 mins. Add remaining ingredients, cook starter over the top for 10 mins. Cook pineapple for dessert, keep warm. Unmould crème caramels, decorate and serve.	Remove Paella from heat, place in serving dish, keep warm. Serve Courgette starter, followed by the Paella and then the Crème Caramel desserts.

MENU 4

● Spicy Beetroots with Orange ● Cod Focaccia ● Hot Mango and Kiwi with Ginger

2 hrs	45 mins	30 mins	15 mins
Prepare the cod for main course, cover and marinate, turning occasionally. Prepare the tomatoes and olives and reserve.	Prepare the starter for cooking. Prepare dessert for cooking, place in parcels and seal. Slice the focaccia for the main course.	Set beetroots to steam for 15 mins over dressing. Remove, peel and slice, place in serving dish. Transfer dressing, to a small pan. ● Remove fish from marinade, place in steamer with tomatoes and olives.	Set steamer to boil. Cook fish for 10–15 mins. Keep warm. Fry focaccia in butter and oil and keep warm. Heat dressing for beetroots, pour over and serve. Serve the fish and focaccia. Set the dessert to steam while eating main course.

MENU 5

● Mediterranean Artichokes ● Pasta Primavera ● Apricot Custard with Caramel Sauce

3 hrs	45 mins–1 hr	35–40 mins	30 mins
Prepare, steam and chill the dessert until ready to serve.	Prepare the ingredients for the starter, place in a foil parcel. Reserve.	Prepare the vegetables for the pasta and place in a steamer tier. Set salted water to boil in steamer base for the pasta.	Set artichokes to steam for 20 mins. Remove and serve onto warm plates. Put pasta in the steamer base and cook vegetables over the top for 10 mins while serving starter. Drain pasta and keep warm. Top with vegetables and serve. ● Unmould the dessert, decorate and serve.

MENU 6

● Scallops in Creamy Saffron Sauce ● Lamb with Port and Garlic ● Charlotte Russe

4 hrs	1½ hrs	20 mins	10 mins
Soak the pears for the dessert for 20 mins. Prepare custard and line the mould. Assemble dessert, cover and steam for 40–50 mins. Chill completely in the refrigerator.	Prepare the scallops, marinate for 1 hr, turning occasionally. Place lamb in marinade. Cover and marinate for 1 hr, turning occasionally.	Place lamb sauce ingredients in a small pan. Set the steamer to boil. Remove the scallops from the marinade and place in steamer tier. Place sauce ingredients in a small pan. Make brandy cream for the dessert if serving.	Set the scallops to steam and the sauce to heat, serve as the starter. While serving scallops, set the lamb to cook, for 15–20 mins. Heat the sauce to serve. ● Serve lamb garnished with rosemary. ● Invert dessert and serve with brandy cream.

INDEX